Selldorf
Architects

Selldorf
Architects

Portfolio
and Projects

Foreword

W. I. Van Campen

Over the thirty years I have known Annabelle Selldorf, she has developed a prolific and diverse architectural practice based in New York City. Born and raised in Cologne, Germany—her father was an architect originally trained as a furniture designer and a craftsman—she came to New York to pursue her professional education at Pratt Institute, where she was inspired by Raimund Abraham's passion for authenticity. Her graduate studies under Colin Rowe at Syracuse University in Florence sharpened her connoisseurship and interest in the social nature of space. An apprenticeship with Richard Gluckman gained her experience with art-related projects prior to founding her independent practice, in 1988. From a modest start with an office of one—Annabelle herself—Selldorf Architects now numbers some sixty-five people, and it is the tremendous collective effort of the partners, staff, and other collaborators that produces the singularly consistent work.

The oeuvre's distinctive sensibility, however, cannot be straight-forwardly explained by Annabelle's early influences. Her work exists at the nexus of many vectors—including the Old and New Worlds, construction and decoration, art and commerce—but actually stands apart in their interstices. Eschewing conceptual abstraction, she elevates function and tactility of materials. Instead of gratuitous formalism, she proposes limpid and well-proportioned spaces. She responds to context with subtle allusion rather than mimetic reference. Taken individually, these tropes are not uncommon to other architects— but taken as a whole, they are recognizable as a unique voice.

This alchemy is not easily decoded, but two clues may provide guidance. First, in many ways Annabelle is a descendant of the great Viennese architect Adolf Loos. In the dialectic he formulated between classical form and utilitarian appointments, Loos found a path both intell-ectually compelling and practically useful. Annabelle has adopted and extended this to provide herself a methodology both rigorous and flexible enough to deal with the exigencies of contemporary commissions. At the same time, where Loos argued against the concept of *Gesamtkunstwerk*, Selldorf always tries to synthesize different design aspects into a totality.

However, this never feels controlled—again, by managing the feat of being simultaneously Loosian and anti-Loosian, she characteristically distinguishes herself.

The second clue may be found in Annabelle's intrinsic *taste*—commonly misunderstood as subjective preference. Most architects assume they have good taste—but in reality it is no longer part of their formal training, and it is quite rare. In Annabelle's mind, it reassumes the traditional virtue of discerning quality and appropriateness, depending on each unique situation. To a great extent, the focused cultivation of this ability is what separates her from her peers.

W. I. Van Campen is an architect in private practice in New York.

Conversation

Tom Eccles and Annabelle Selldorf

Tom Eccles: As an architect, you came to prominence with a strong association between, and an affinity for, art and architecture. What was your first experience of art and architecture? I imagine it was as a young girl in a church in Germany?

Annabelle Selldorf: I grew up in the later postwar era in the sixties in Cologne, Germany. My parents were architects/designers and had many close artist friends—I grew up amongst them, looking at their work in exhibitions and in their studios. When we were kids, my parents took us along to visit exhibitions, to museums, art openings, and the like. The topic of architecture was not discussed as a distinct discipline, but certainly I remember going to see buildings—mostly museums— and developing a sense of architecture through the eyes of my parents. Growing up in the sixties in a period still of rebuilding a much-destroyed Cologne, all architecture was modern and under the influence of the Bauhaus. It was the vocabulary of contemporary building. You speak of churches: while we were not religious, Cologne has many great Romanesque churches and, of course, the great Gothic cathedral, the dome to Cologne. I cannot say for sure that looking at churches influenced my sense of space—but I rather like the idea.

TE   Has art replaced religion? Should galleries and museums be cathedrals? Are you an architect for the agnostic?

AS   To the extent that art can provide moments of transcendence, I think it can be likened to a religious experience—for some. We create and assign spaces to enable the experience of such transcendence, and traditionally art and architecture have done this in unison. Think of the great Renaissance churches or Gothic cathedrals with their paintings, stained glass, and sculptures in grand and overwhelming spaces. I think that this sense of awe is just as possible in modern architecture— Louis Kahn's Kimbell Art Museum, for example. It is a place of such a finely articulated volume juxtaposed with an elegant palette of materials and a subtle wash of daylight that it only ever complements and never distracts from looking at art. Architecture is not for the believers or the nonbelievers. Architecture should be powerful on its own—dignify and elevate its purpose, in the Vitruvian sense: *firmitas, utilitas, venustas*, or solid, useful, and beautiful.

TE   That's as agnostic an answer as you can probably get! What do you mean by "architecture should elevate its purpose"?

AS   What I mean is that it should be thoroughly conceived such that nothing needs to be added or subtracted, ultimately making space dedicated to clarity and light and well-being.

TE   You're starting to sound a little like Adolf Loos in *Ornament and Crime*! For you, where is the boundary between art and architecture? Where do they overlap, run parallel, diverge? Your buildings seem to maintain a very respectful distinction or at least restraint with regard to where architecture ends and art can exist.

AS   I am not sure that a distinct boundary exists: architecture is art. As a matter of fact, it is the *mother* of all arts. . . . The art of architecture is subject to different considerations, however, from those that inform the visual arts, I suspect, because while we—architects—begin with the notion of serving a utilitarian purpose, the thesis of architecture is of a different nature. All arts, in their own way, have to push boundaries, attempt to fulfill their thesis, and excel in doing so such that the experience of it offers resonance. Apropos of resonance, there is a famed Palladio theater in Vicenza: what is remarkable about it is that the acoustics in the amphitheater are so good that sitting in the last row you can hear a person speaking in a normal timbre on stage. Just to say that the great elegance of the design would be nil if it were not also for the incredible performance of the building.

TE   In a number of recent articles and interviews, your work has been compared to, and you yourself compare it to, "slow food." In fact, you have said, "I feel like I'm the equivalent of slow food in architecture. What we do isn't spectacular. Unless perhaps it's a slow spectacle." What does that mean?

9

AS   Our work is seldom about spectacular gestures but rather about a series of decisions that come together and pertain to structure, proportion, light, and specific use, the strength of which reveal themselves more gradually. On another, level it refers to the speed of my brain. . . .

TE   I thought you might be referencing a kind of Arts and Crafts movement, a resistance to acceleration and perhaps a whiff of "taste." A response to accelerated capitalism, and initially a reaction to a proposed McDonald's at the foot of the Spanish Steps in Rome, the slow-food movement proposes "sensual pleasure and slow, long-lasting enjoyment." "Knowledge" and "discernment" are other qualities of the cooking school of thought. I wonder if the analogy worries you? Perhaps that's too aggressive.

AS   Aggressive indeed—"Arts and Crafts," "taste. . . ." These are big words that conjure connotations that I do not like so much. And then when you go on to "knowledge" and "discernment," I get very nervous—absolutely! Enough with the analogies! Certainly, though, there is a banalization that has happened to architecture as a result of a culture that is almost exclusively based on images, so abundant and out of context that the quick impression is all there is. It does not seem that permanence or longevity are any longer given their due value, and so that has changed the paradigm.

TE   You are famous for, among other things, the design of David Zwirner's gallery in Chelsea that exemplifies a heightened sense of auratic experience. You've been perhaps unfairly associated with a Minimalist approach to organizing space, or at the very least having a restrained approach to architecture. I know you've said you don't want to be Donald Judd or Richard Serra, but how would you describe your work in relation to Minimalist strategies?

AS   I think that strategies in architecture address fundamentally different conditions than those in art. Perhaps it could be said that they have to serve a wider set of circumstances and references, for that matter. Minimalism in architecture has become a question of style, which I am not very interested in. I believe that we always have to start with utilitarian purpose; obviously, that is not enough, though. There has to be an idea—it includes how and for what purpose people use space, but more importantly, how they experience it. It seems to me that finding a very narrow path where an intervention does as little as is necessary—never too much but enough to be monumental—is a goal. To that end, analysis and quest for resolution is the means: somehow it is about a very rational approach that is rigorously subjective, if that makes any sense. This reminds me of a saying—I think it was by Albert Einstein—"Make everything as simple as possible but not simpler."

TE   Maybe you could unpack some of those concepts in real terms, say in regards to David Zwirner Gallery? What is rational, subjective, and utilitarian about David Zwirner Gallery?

AS   David Zwirner's building is a good example of all that is in my mind. To begin with, there was a definition of the spaces and their attributes. It was evident that the central need was to provide a large and tall, column-free exhibition space that would be mostly lit with daylight, yet with flexibility to be divided into different configurations to serve different kinds of art and other aspects of the program: more exhibition space on the second floor, showrooms, a kitchen for those working in the building, etc., could all be rationally organized. But the choices that pertain to how the structure is expressed, the juxtaposition of varying proportions and exposure to differently orientated windows together with a concrete staircase winding upward in a tall skylit space, as well as the choices of few materials, are subjective and willful decisions. Yet I view them as a deliberate attempt to get to that tenuous balance of doing nothing too much but not failing on account of "not enough." I think of the building as a whole that occupies a tight spot in an urban context, and therefore the facade is an exercise of the same balance.

TE   I think that could probably be said of many of your projects, including the Neue Galerie in New York, for which you renovated a 1914 Carrère & Hastings Fifth Avenue mansion into a museum for Ronald Lauder's collection of early-twentieth-century German and Austrian art, including Gustav Klimt's famous *Portrait of Adele Bloch-Bauer I*. Or Hauser & Wirth in Piccadilly, with the transformation of a 1923 bank building by Sir Edwin Lutyens—what you have called "a jewel box of a building." In both cases, there is an astonishing level of restraint on your part. What makes these Selldorf buildings today? Where is your signature?

AS   The question about signature is always interesting, because it is about the difference between legibility and individual imprint.

I don't perceive it to be my responsibility or my objective to provide the "easy-to-recognize" attribute, though I believe that there is a distinct handwriting in our work. Naturally, in projects that are more about renovation/restoration or repurposing I prefer an attitude of restraint, whereas in new construction it is more possible to establish a proprietary vocabulary. Or a grammar that answers to its own rules, as it were. In all cases—new construction or renovation—it always comes back to trying to find a path of resolution and clarity. When we were tasked to design a recycling facility in Sunset Park, Brooklyn, there was just an empty pier, the site on which this industrial facility was to be located. Accepting certain basic operational requirements, the placement, size, and relationship of building components to one another became the generator for a set of hierarchies. It was the juxtaposition of these with a series of indoor and outdoor spaces in dialogue with one another as well as introducing a circulatory spine along the north side of the pier, paired with a simple singular material aesthetic, that created a monumental yet peaceful environment. And this is what I think of as our signature.

TE   What do you think about the phenomena of "starchitects"?

AS   I wonder who came up with this word in the first place. It does not contribute anything qualitative. It certainly does not say anything good. Is a starchitect similar to a starlet? It is a word full of innuendo, but I am not sure to what end—to condemn architecture as a whole or just the architects to whom this label is attached. I remember when Richard Meier did the apartment buildings on West Street and Perry Street, people became interested in the fact that developers had hired a well-known architect—a starchitect. I thought that this actually represented a positive trend in commercial architecture: developers hiring an architect known to design buildings of a certain quality rather than an unknown licensed professional to build the least expensive building with the most square footage. It got more complicated, though, because then architects became part of the "branding" for buildings, and quickly the "starchitect" word was entirely pejorative.

TE   Architects working globally have to confront the realities of local conditions such as labor practices and the treatment or mistreatment of migrant workers. This does, though, raise the question of ethics and responsibility among today's leading architects. Do you think they are any different from, say, multinational corporations with their own particular brands to maintain, etc.?

AS   The broader, more philosophical, question is, to what extent is an architect divorced from the context and merely charged with practicing his or her craft? It seems to me that there has to be some correlation between the two. It is worrisome that large commissions around the world get realized by well-known architects, and yet transgressions are taciturnly overlooked. While it may not be the architect's role to negotiate labor conditions, it seems that the status of lead architect offers an opportunity to be outspoken and to direct the eye of the public to unacceptable conditions. Needless to say, any public criticism by the architect may come at the cost of those commissions, which presumably explains the lack of any vocal outreach. While there are differences between the multinational corporation and the lead architect—the corporations actively negotiate the conditions, whereas the architect may have little authority, perhaps only a voice with the public—ethical responsibility exists for both.

TE   Architecture is by its very nature a collaborative process. For you, what is the nature of that collaboration?

AS   Indeed, I agree that architecture is collaborative by nature. It is not always viewed that way. Quite the opposite; often, architecture is perceived to be conceived as a solitary creative process. For me, collaboration is total. While I bring my own aspiration, creative aesthetic, and point of view to it, collaboration infuses every aspect of the process. It all starts with establishing a relationship of give-and-take with the client; then, there is the working relationship within our own team, when everyone brings their talent and intelligence to the design process. I cannot imagine not working closely with my partners, Sara Lopergolo, Julie Hausch-Fen, Lisa Green, and Bill Bigelow. We have been working together for many years now, and it is a tremendous experience to have the kind of trust and confidence we gain from working with one another. And then, there is a host of others who contribute their expertise to realize a project. Adversity rears its ugly head when collaboration doesn't happen, when information doesn't flow and people work at cross-purposes. Then, many things can go wrong, and terrible mistakes and strife happen. Everybody has had that experience. Fostering a culture of collaboration has been one of the most important lessons I have learned.

TE   What is your methodology for working with clients?

AS   First, we listen and get to know the client; we find out everything there is to know about a project, learn to understand the conditions, the particulars of site, program, expectation, trajectory, etc. Then, we work. This means absorbing all that you have learned, and in the end formulating an idea. From there, it evolves through an iterative process to arrive at the inevitable. Sometimes, this process is seemingly without effort—but not always. At times, it seems like there is a great deal of psychological and diplomatic skill, and a healthy dose of stubbornness, involved in guiding the process of design. These days, clients rely on the prompt delivery of images, and this sometimes stifles our process, for we cannot deliver a ready-made object available for distribution pulled out of a drawer at the onset of a project. Of course, this goes back to what constitutes a ready signature look. Instead, our method is predicated on complete immersion in a given problem, with dedication to its many folds and with numerous iterations until a unique idea emerges where the purposeful and the poetic meet in seeming effortlessness.

TE   We live in a time that seems to privilege the artist, and artists are often given a voice and authority in areas that would have been traditionally beyond their purview and may in fact lie outside their skill set. This is probably a hangover from the sixties and seventies, when architecture inflicted some rather dreadful conditions on the lived environment, and the artist became a kind of panacea or at least tempering element to humanize the built environment. Do you think this is an effective role for artists?

AS   Generally speaking, I believe that any time art is given influence, that is a very good thing; while I believe that art and architecture are closely interrelated, visual art is not architecture, and often an artist's purview over matters of architecture does not address the larger issues at stake—and indeed, their intervention serves just as a Band-Aid when more radical surgery is required. Very often, an artist's contribution was reduced to mere application on a building after the design was complete as "public art"—sometimes required by public financing—and then is effective for neither art nor architecture. On the south side of Union Square, across from our office, there is a large developer building from the late 1990s of no particular quality, but it is not helped in any way by the somewhat overwrought artist's installation, *Metronome*. Though, when artists and architects push the envelope to motivate a different thinking about structure and society, that is often where interesting things and real collaborations become possible. I am thinking of the inclusive and multidisciplinary discourse going on at Luma, Arles.

TE   In an age when the public and private are essentially blurred, can architecture clarify, or does it mask the difference between the two?

AS   This is damn hard to answer, and I am not sure how to tackle it. Where to begin? Everybody talks about public space—where in spatial terms the blur of public and private happens—and what it has to deliver. Nothing interests me more. The role of architecture is in large measure to support the harmony between public and private space. Public space has become synonymous with "available to everybody," which then in turn often means that it can only be less specific and consequently precludes a sense of privacy or intimacy or focus. It gets very complicated very quickly, though I believe that articulating differentiated spheres without accepting exclusivity as a trade-off is entirely possible. But then we'll have to get more concrete.

TE   Architecture often rubs up against the public. What role do you see for community involvement in decisions that affect their environment?

AS   There are numerous agencies that represent the interests of the public, though those may not always fully capture the entire interests of the community and can get mired in the political process. So it is particularly important for architects to provide opportunity for direct interaction with the communities that will be served. And how is it that we as architects are meant to deal with issues of gentrification, with "not in my backyard," with rising tides, overcrowding, violence, dilapidated infrastructure, and the many other topics that don't have a simple solution? While there may be no short answer, I consider it part of our obligation and intent to be committed to hearing the discordant voices and to being sensitive and cognizant of them. It is our reason for being to create a built environment that serves humanity and civilization, no matter how messy.

TE   You recently completed the Sims Municipal Recycling facility in Sunset Park, Brooklyn, a surprisingly utilitarian commission for you. It suggests the possibility for a much broader set of building types.

What kinds of projects have you not yet realized? In more general terms, what do you see as the trajectory of your practice?

AS   When we were asked to design the recycling facility, it was a chance to envision an industrial operation as also a place for people, and a piece of public infrastructure, where design could have a real impact. This was very appealing about the brief. We have just begun working on a not-for-profit project for a school for children in Mwabwindo, Zambia. How could one not take great pleasure and satisfaction contributing to something so desperately needed? The pleasure is only amplified by the enthusiasm of my colleagues in our office for this project. More than a particular type of building, I am most happy to be working on projects where the public comes together and that create an enriching experience for people, whether that be a museum, a library, an auditorium, or a place of introspection and discovery.

This conversation expands on one between Tom Eccles and Annabelle Selldorf published in *ArtReview 66*, no. 9 (December 2014). Tom Eccles is the executive director of the Center for Curatorial Studies at Bard College, Annandale-on-Hudson, New York.

Portfolio

Sims Sunset Park Material Recovery Facility

Sims Sunset Park Material Recovery Facility

Skarstedt Residence

Sims Sunset Park Material Recovery Facility

Skarstedt Residence

Berg'n

David Zwirner, 20th Street

Skarstedt Residence

David Zwirner, 20th Street

200 Eleventh Avenue

Chelsea Townhouse

Sims Sunset Park Material Recovery Facility

Skarstedt Residence

Walden House

House in the Springs

520 West Chelsea

Hauser & Wirth, 18th Street

Clark Art Institute

415 West 13th Street

Tobias Meyer Office, Seagram Building

10 Bond Street

David Zwirner, 20th Street

David Zwirner, 20th Street

Walden House

David Zwirner, 20th Street

Skarstedt Residence

David Zwirner, 20th Street

200 Eleventh Avenue

Neue Galerie

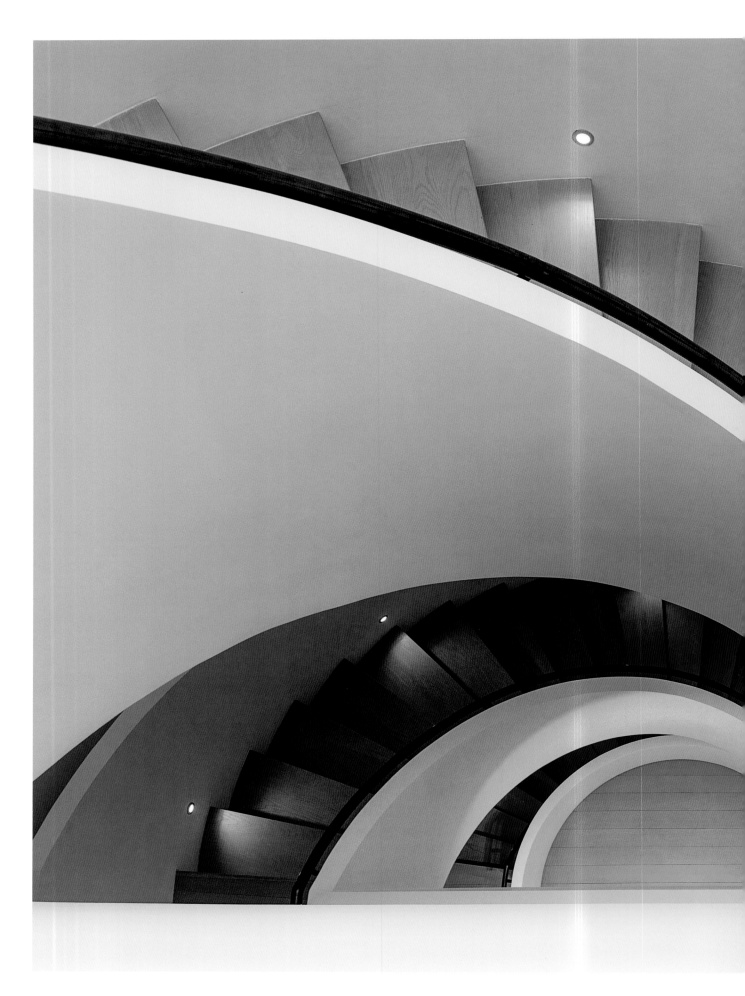

Chelsea Townhouse

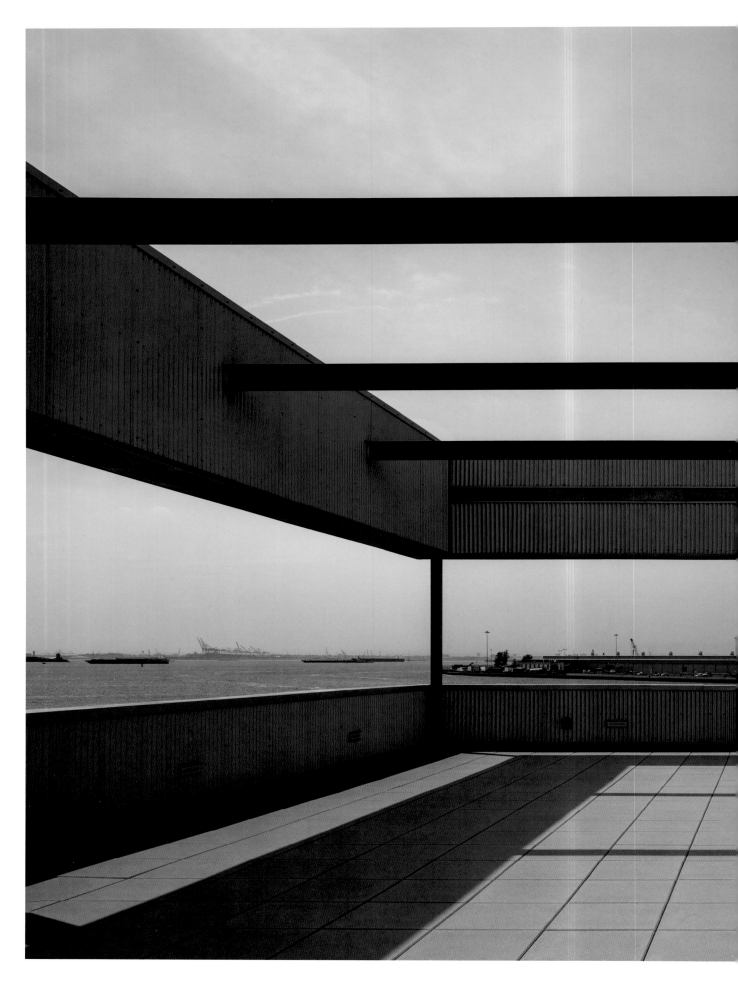

Sims Sunset Park Material Recovery Facility

Clark Art Institute

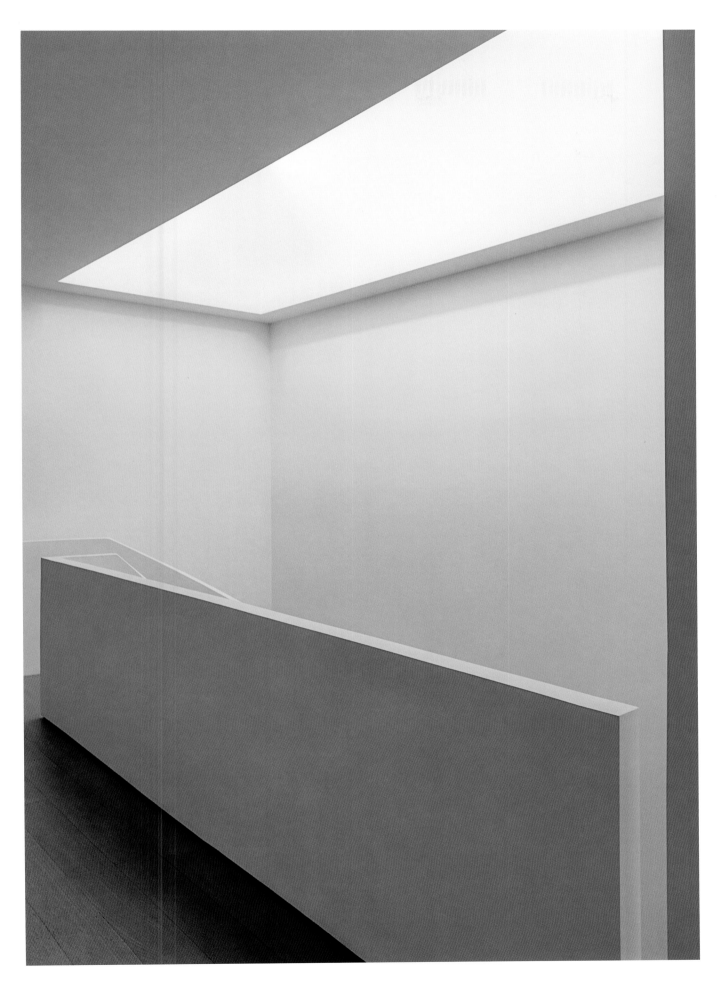

Chelsea Townhouse

Hauser & Wirth, 69th Street

Hauser & Wirth, 18th Street

Sims Sunset Park Material Recovery Facility

VeneKlasen Carriage House

Clark Art Institute

David Zwirner, 20th Street

Van de Weghe Townhouse

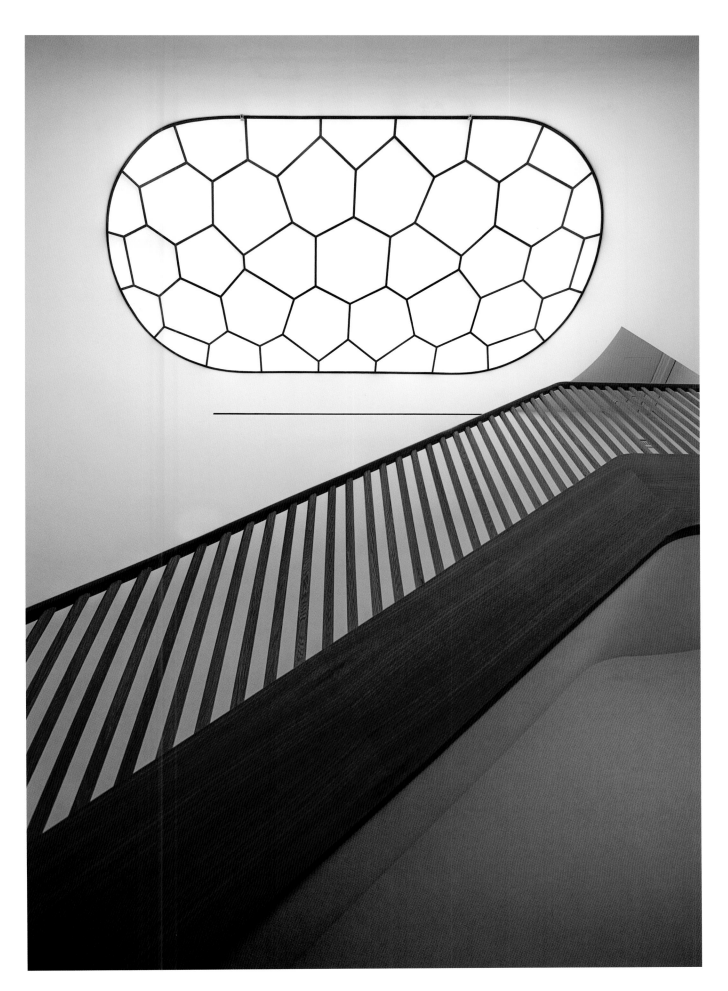

Van de Weghe Townhouse

Skarstedt Residence

Walden House

House in the Springs

VeneKlasen Carriage House

Sims Sunset Park Material Recovery Facility

10 Bond Street

10 Bond Street

John Hay Library

Chelsea Townhouse

520 West Chelsea

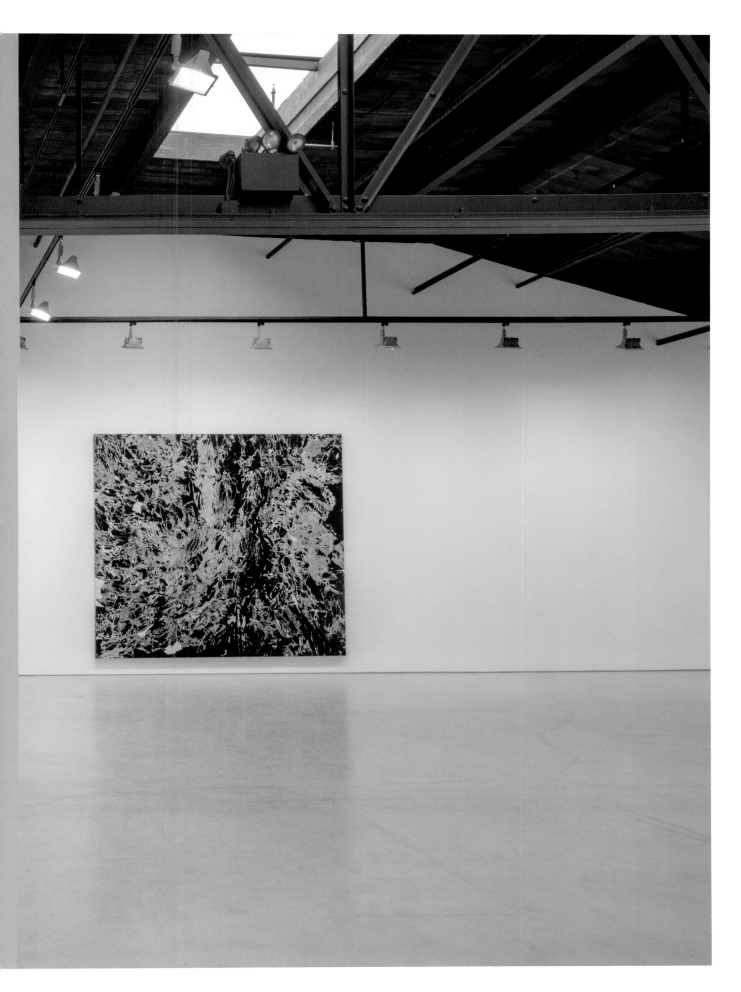

Hauser & Wirth, 18th Street

Clark Art Institute

David Zwirner, 20th Street

Neue Galerie

Upper West Side Apartment

VeneKlasen Carriage House

Clark Art Institute

Upper West Side Apartment

Van de Weghe Townhouse

David Zwirner, 19th Street

Van de Weghe Townhouse

Upper West Side Apartment

Skarstedt Residence

Sims Sunset Park Material Recovery Facility

Walden House

John Hay Library

Neue Galerie

John Hay Library

Gladstone Gallery, 21st Street

House in the Springs

Skarstedt Residence

10 Bond Street

David Zwirner, 20th Street

Essential Architecture

Ian Volner

Selldorf Architects is a firm unlike any other in the design world today, and writing about it means tossing out some of the typical gear in the critical toolbox.

For starters, the office's work is uniquely resistant to easy visual metaphors or expository prose. The probing, seeking nature of its approach—of which more to follow—makes each building more and more *itself*, adhering to its own internal logic; what connects the projects is precisely that they do not impose, upon the end user, the kind of rhetorical program easily elaborated upon by the critic. Many observers have commented on the primacy of personal experience as a prerequisite to truly understanding a work of architecture, and that goes double in this instance: the impulse is to want to place the reader in one of the firm's buildings and simply say, "Look."

Likewise, the office's position in the field of contemporary architecture, which also defies simple categorization. Clients have turned to the firm for architectural statements whose subtlety is their strength. Even among designers operating in a more outré vein, Selldorf Architects commands considerable respect, and it reflects it back again in its thoughtful, deferential buildings. There is a critical aspect embedded in the practice—more on that subject as well—but it's a form of critique that begins by renouncing polemics almost completely. The near silence of Selldorf Architects' buildings speaks volumes.

Indeed, it's precisely in its seeming quietude that Selldorf Architects does find a language, a communicative mode that responds to one of architecture's most daunting problems.

To put it bluntly, many people, even otherwise culturally attuned ones, don't *get architecture*. The poetics of space; the romance of materials both organic and synthetic; "the correct and magnificent play of masses brought together in light," as Le Corbusier put it—the basic phenomenological constituents of modern architecture often fail, and fail badly, to translate into a generally understood idiom. The most impressive, expressive architectural assemblages often elicit merely a kind of stumped incredulity, while the most polished and platonically reductive ones provoke, at best, a bored shrug. Somehow, this most essential of arts—the one type of cultural production that is a predicate to almost all the others, and which provides housing and offices and recreational spaces to the entire developed world—has come, in our time, to seem a bit of a cipher.

This is the condition that Selldorf Architects has inherited, and that it seems determined to challenge. Architecture, the orphan of the arts. Designers trapped between the banality of gesture and the banality of the service profession. Where is the line of flight?

Time Life

The house opens up like a book. Immediately there is the broad vista, the billiard-baize lawn, and the suggestion of a sea that almost appears to be the subject of an exhibition—which, in a sense, it is. For this is a house for art, and the rooms at the rear are arranged in a symmetrical sequence as if, in a *grand palais*, some American genie had ripped off a wall to let in the summer. The upper floors mirror the lower, only halved and enclosed, and with a deferential attitude to the landscape that seems to compose a pastoral essay on the virtue of unseasonable cloud cover as a chastened version of the Good Life. The disposition of space in every sense: a system with a mood. "The heart," Pascal wrote, "has its reasons which reason knows nothing of." But reason, it turns out, is also a heart.

"Si discorda tutta quella musica"

In the twenty-seven years that she's been in practice, Annabelle Selldorf hasn't been the only one trying to reconnect architecture to its audience. But the way she's threaded that particular needle, as well as her results, have set her apart.

Selldorf's uniquely varied formation as an architect has made her well suited to the task. Born in Cologne, Selldorf came of age in a country still recovering from the ravages of World War II; Mies and the Bauhaus represented, for her generation, a way forward, an escape from the mistakes of the past. Moving to New York in the late 1970s to study at Pratt, she encountered a very different architectural milieu. Under the tutelage of teachers such as Colin Rowe and Raimund Abraham, Selldorf found architecture in a state of flux, with Modernism as it had been practiced theretofore undergoing a radical reconsideration.

The reasons for this had precisely to do with the long-standing language barrier between design and its audience. The clean lines and unadorned surfaces of the dominant International Style had come, on these shores at least, to be perceived by many as confining, sterile, even authoritarian; their delicate pleasures had always been a bit obscure to nonspecialists, prompting Tom Wolfe, in his 1981 polemic *From Bauhaus to Our House*, to wonder why "so many people of wealth and power have paid for and put up with so much architecture they detested." Selldorf's arrival coincided almost precisely with the advent of what Jean-Louis Cohen has called "that hesitation in practice," the Postmodernist movement, which had as its explicit goal the recovery of an architectural vocabulary rooted in history and popular culture. Its effects were salutary in many ways, but ultimately it couldn't sustain its early momentum and fell into critical and popular disfavor.

The formal tendency that was announced in the late 1980s, and that assumed its present ascendancy beginning with Frank Gehry's Guggenheim Bilbao in 1997, attempted to break through the discursive static by amplifying the language of Modernism, stretching materials and forms almost to the breaking point. This trend has produced some of the true architectural masterworks of our time—but just like Modernism (and then Postmodernism), it too has produced a feeling of fatigue in some quarters, especially among that large segment of the public that feels intimidated or bewildered by capital-D Design. Once again comes the feeling of alienation. Less may not always be more. But then again, neither is more.

Selldorf Architects, however, has managed to turn this double bind into a generative constraint. For the last three decades, it has played its own, ingeniously improvised riff over and against the dominant strains of the profession. The firm's keynote could be described as an objectivity of affect: a reflexive attitude, calm and assured and agnostic, that underwrites its carefully focused design process, enabling it to step back to evaluate its products.

It's a procedure that unfolds as a steady winnowing away of uncertainties and externalities. Contrary to the highly finished, resolved quality of the completed projects, the Selldorf team does not as a general rule begin with firm convictions about the materials, the detailing, or the overall envelope of their projects; these, which would appear to be the most eminent aspects of any building, are developed only after a long consideration of a host of factors—not just functional but financial, urbanistic, even infrastructural—to arrive at a general sense of the objectives of the project. Naturally, this makes for a heavy reliance on collaboration, drawing on input and expertise from clients and consultants, and it's no coincidence that Selldorf Architects has become a go-to firm for sensitive commissions requiring a special kind of architectural diplomacy. Whether it be the renovation of a beloved historical landmark (such as the Neue Galerie), the construction of an apartment complex cheek by jowl with its neighbors (such as 10 Bond Street), or the creation of living spaces for creative clients with their own pronounced sense of taste (as in the homes for prominent art-world figures), the studio's highly deliberative process allows for a degree of flexibility to ensure that the result reflects all the competing interests that informed it. As adaptable as it is, however, Selldorf Architects' process is remarkable for how few real variations or digressions it seems to entail. This, again, attests to the affective approach that guides the studio's method from the beginning and—still more important—at the end. In the final design phase, as the necessary decisions about basic aesthetic considerations are being made, purely analytical criteria are set aside to some degree; an innate *sense* of rational order takes over from rigorous rational *practice*, and the ultimate design choices are guided almost by a feeling of inevitability. Proceeding from logic to intuition, the designer declines the role of all-commanding demiurge, and the end user profits by having the conviction that the space truly belongs to him or her.

An architecture of the door handle, of the precisely articulated lintel, of the finely turned brass banister and well-tempered steel trellis—change anything, Alberti warned, and "throw all that music into discord"! But walk away from it, turn around and go on with the day: the music recedes into ambience. The devil is in the details. Why not leave him there.

City Life

> This muck heaves and palpitates. It is multi-directional and has a mayor. —Donald Barthelme, *City Life*, 1970

There is a copper-colored vessel in the middle of town. It arrived quite suddenly one day, less as though it had been placed there than as though the city had simply yielded it, like a fruit. At first, there was lively debate as to the copper-ness—was it raw copper, or burnt? Was it carmine? Ancient sunset, umber, Tuscan hillside in September. . . . Some moved to call it sienna, but this is rank provocation. No, it's definitely copper-colored. And it's definitely a vessel, though this too causes some confusion, for it appears to billow; the edges are diaphanous; it is decked out in unfamiliar padding. Ribbands, perhaps. Or bolstered, as a chaise in a European hotel. Yes, bolstered. In the middle of town, the copper-colored vessel, as we call it, composes itself with democratic ease: cars and candy wrappers, restaurant equipment, children with plastic bats—all the willful dejecta of the metropolis—these it gathers up only to roll them out again, giving them back to themselves. They accept it in the spirit of the gift, and this is tremendous, the effect being that we are almost unaware of it. For that is all we want, we put-upon citizens: buffeted by bicyclists and conventioneers, all we want is something that is like the city itself, red and invaluable, a vessel, so that we may walk past it and be reminded of nothing except that *we are where we always meant to be*. It is one of us, this new entity. The city coalesces around it, and it creates a wild civility.

The Machine in the Garden in the Machine

Though frequently Minimalistic, Annabelle Selldorf is emphatically not a Minimalist. This conceptual distinction is essential to understanding her studio's work, in particular its buildings for the viewing of art, which have been central to Selldorf Architects' portfolio since the firm's early Manhattan gallery projects.

The David Zwirner gallery on West 20th Street in Manhattan is a perfect case study. The necessarily neutral character of the interior is quietly undermined by the superbly grained concrete, the wood finishes, and, of course, the dim and perilously tall-seeming staircase winding among the floors (staircases being, in the Selldorf oeuvre, a frequent moment of drama). Given the range of contemporary artistic practice, which tends increasingly toward large-scale installations, the requirements for displaying it involve a unique resistance to theatricality—including the theatricality of restraint. The gallery's inaugural exhibition in 2013, featuring the work of Donald Judd alongside that of Dan Flavin, made lucid just how much Selldorf's work differs from full-blown artistic Minimalism: the artworks on view seemed to stand out all the more for being in a space that does not attempt to vie with them for evocative asceticism.

A similar tactic is deployed in the Clark Art Institute, a project that also shows Selldorf Architects engaged in what has become one of its core competencies: the renovation and transformation of preexisting structures. Again, as in its domestic work, the organization of space is highly rationalized, the architectural promenade unfolding with an almost classical rigor; again, as in its urban projects, the response to context—in this case, the original Neo-Classical structure, the adjacent new building by Tadao Ando, and the orderly pastoralism of Reed Hilderbrand's landscape design—alternates between mediation and deflection, becoming part of the whole while still maintaining a logic of its own. More than any other typology, the museum has become the favored repository of designers' most ambitious attempts to establish architecture's disciplinary autonomy. Selldorf Architects' prudent ambivalence on that subject is what gives its museum and gallery work its sense of candor, its unfussy charm.

None of this is to diminish the amount of attention that the studio invests in its work, or the attention that the work rewards. Certainly, we are invited to consider at length the exquisite surface treatments and carefully calibrated spaces of buildings such as the Walden House, the Gladstone Gallery, and even the Sims Sunset Park Material Recovery Facility. But the untempered enthusiasm for form that underlies both architectural maximalism and minimalism is alien to Selldorf Architects' measured cool. The essence of its casual refinement is that it becomes the object of contemplation only when we choose for it to be so. In an age of skepticism, the firm's is an architecture of circumspect beauty.

A formalism against formalism: the lyrical giving way to the logical, or vice versa. Within the factory, the mansion: inside the mansion, the factory. Or vice versa. Or both simultaneously, or mise en abyme. . . . Or neither.

Past Predicate

The representation of history . . . requires a falsification of perspective. —W. G. Sebald, *The Rings of Saturn*, 1995

In the middle of an otherwise normal 2001, someone has placed a spectacular dresser studded in shimmering 1914. Downstairs, the shadows are lengthening in the gathering late-Romanticism, and the chef is serving a large Vienna to a group of appreciative fall collection (definitely pre-Revolution); the visitors ascend a tightly packed Information Age, then enter into the Tiergarten on a sunny afternoon, the height of the hurricane season and the air charged with a distinct Diaghilev. Yes, there it is before them—an enormous purple folk music, ringed in plaster, inlaid with gold, the work of a prominent Gothic engraver turned Jewish sex symbol and occasional picture postcard. How did all this come about? Like this: the past has to recede from itself in order to be understood. The guiding hand is that of a European of the classic downtown post-punk scene, so there is little doubt that history isn't being so much "used" here as held in abeyance, invited to stay, laughed at with good-natured opprobrium, and then asked back for a subsequent interview. The vestibule is still a vestibule, but the robber baron has been replaced by a coat rack. Bottle after bottle of 1926.

Everything New Is Old Again

For all her comfort with history, Annabelle Selldorf obviously maintains a staunch affiliation with the project of modernity. But not an uncritical one, nor one uninflected by other varieties of experience, other modalities.

The Sims Sunset Park Material Recovery Facility, simply by dint of its industrial character, instantly puts one in mind of some of the great monuments of early architectural Modernism—Gropius's Fagus-Werk springs to mind. The project, as *New York Times* architecture critic Michael Kimmelman said, is "an architectural keeper," one that adds "an improbable grace note to a gritty stretch of Brooklyn." But look again: as such notes go, this one has a most gritty grace, and from the catwalks surrounding the main processing floor the visitor is treated to a spectacle of raw function that is miles from Gropius's tranquil ensemble. Selldorf is quite content to let the building be both composed and messy, its delicate massing juxtaposed with its rough-and-ready, off-the-shelf materiality. The civic value that Kimmelman rightly praises isn't so much celebrated by the building as frankly assumed by it. Monumentality, except of the most subdued sort, is not in the Selldorf playbook.

Functionalism, of course, has always been a central theme in modernism, and certainly Selldorf may be called a functionalist. But the elevation or brash expression of function is no more to her liking than the preciousness of the more rarified variety of Minimalism, or the extravagance of highly personalized "signature" tropes. Alongside the latter, there has appeared in recent architectural discourse a resurgent and occasionally salutary interest in hyper-functionality—a conviction that new building technologies and advances in energy efficiency, married with a fevered approach to data analysis, can produce a design of almost limitless social potential. About this, too, Selldorf is skeptical, and the lack of messianism evident in her work is part of its critical edge.

Certainly her adherence to Modernism is not a question of (and here we use the dirty word) "style." If anything, the sheer variety of typologies and formal solutions that have proceeded from the office in just the last fifteen years can make it difficult to discern any sort of "Selldorf style," an instantly recognizable aesthetic. This is a reflection of the firm's rather deliberative process: the process, to some degree, is the style. But what I mean to suggest here is that there is something else that makes the firm's projects identifiably its own—that there is a style *behind the process.*

The kind of creative irreverence that marks Selldorf Architects' objective, measured assessment of the prevailing design methodologies of our time, be they formal or functional, seems an extension of Annabelle Selldorf's own character—a convinced urbanite, cosmopolitan in outlook, with a background in the European tradition and a taste for the freewheeling vitality of America. Admittedly, this treads dangerously upon the terrain of the personal—a problematic issue since, as noted, the office goes to great pains not to indulge strictly personal statements. But that's just another one of the intrigues of the practice: its pragmatism and self-effacing cool only underscore the chief commitments of its founder, and the buildings never bear the imprimatur of their creator so clearly as when they are trying their hardest not to.

Even setting aside the question of authorship, the firm's ability to work in so many different registers and to create such a rare breadth of work—without ever manipulating the outward appearance of a building solely to distinguish it from its predecessors—has become itself a kind of calling card. The understated glamour of the Skarstedt Residence, the metropolitan stateliness of 200 Eleventh Avenue, the hip domesticity of the firm's Manhattan apartments: more than just the name on the cover, a sensibility unites the projects cataloged here, and if it takes a moment to recognize it, just keep looking. Out of the aesthetic equilibrium, the almost-offhanded-yet-accomplished handling of every feature and fixture, there emerges a sensation, a feeling of ease strengthened by a critical intelligence.

Several times now I have called Selldorf's practice "critical," and I must be careful to qualify the word. Using it is perhaps inevitable, since so much of this inquiry into the office's work seems to trace a series of negations: not-quite-Minimalist, not-quite-Expressionist; not-formalist, not-functionalist; thoroughly urbanistic, yet never overtly contextual—and, of course, not exclusively poetic, yet somehow inaccessible to analytical methodologies alone. Any practice that weaves so deftly among these dialectical relations has to be called critical, at least provisionally. But the last negation has to be this: that the work of Selldorf Architects, although it is in many ways an "architect's architecture," is not aimed at the profession alone. The diversity of its solutions proves that the firm's real intent is to provide real human service, specific to real human conditions, and to speak to people on their own terms without pandering or pedantry. Rather than the autonomy of architecture, the firm insists on the autonomy of end users, and the restraint that it imposes on itself is the index of the freedom it grants everyone who enters its buildings.

The firm's upcoming projects will find Selldorf Architects operating in more public settings than ever before: the enormous volume of work yet to come ranges from large residential condominiums in New York, to institutional buildings, such as the Museum of Contemporary Art San Diego, to high-end hospitality commissions, such as the Mesa at Amangiri in Utah. It's difficult to reconcile this decidedly modest practice with the scale of work it is now taking on; but to create buildings of every type, for as many people as possible, is part of the Modernist's remit, and Selldorf Architects is not shying away from it. To that mandate the designers are adding the element that makes their work so innovative— the rare quality that promises to bridge the gap, creating an architecture natural to its time and its audience—that improbable mixture of informality and precision that is the firm's own, and that can make its work so forthright and unpresumptuous one moment, yet so absolute and numinous the next.

Projects

Neue Galerie
New York

This extensive renovation transformed a private home built by Carrère & Hastings in 1914 into a museum devoted to German and Austrian art. The practical challenges included adding entrance ramps without detracting from the ornate brick-and-limestone exterior, inserting new mechanical systems without compromising original interior details, and reorganizing the allocation of spaces without disturbing the gracious proportions of the rooms. The reconfigured building provides 5,000 square feet (465 square meters) of gallery space for permanent and temporary exhibitions, as well as a bookstore, design shop, and Viennese-style café. Administrative offices, conservation studios, and archival facilities round out the program on the upper levels.

The entrance ramps are the first sign that the building has been given a new life. Inside, the ground floor was reconfigured to accommodate an elevator and a checkroom. On the second floor, walls were restored or, in the case of the mirrored music room, replaced with recessed plaster panels. On the third floor is an entirely new gallery for changing exhibitions. New elements—such as the ground-floor reception desk and elevator—were designed in a Modernist idiom, clearly announcing their presence as contemporary elements within a historic building.

Building Type: Cultural
Construction Type: Renovation
Size: 23,000 sf (2,137 sm)

Neue Galerie, New York

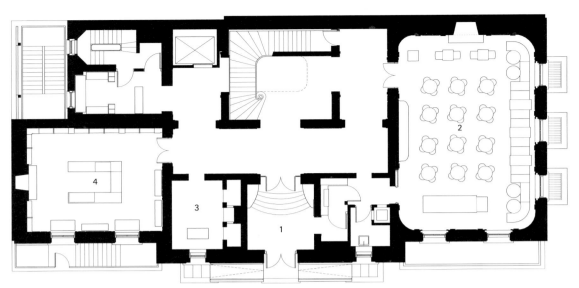

Ground-Floor Plan

1 Entry
2 Café
3 Design Shop
4 Book Shop
5 Gallery

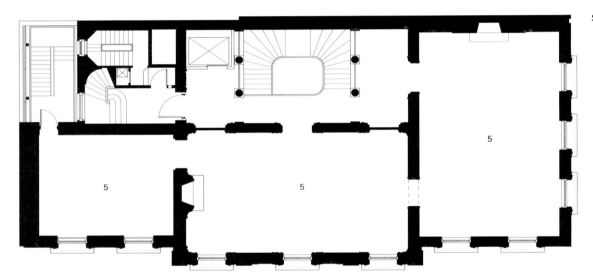

Second-Floor Plan

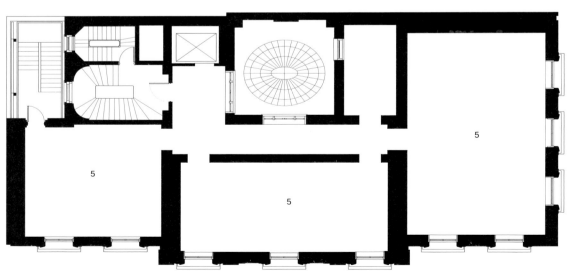

Third-Floor Plan

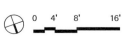

0 4' 8' 16'

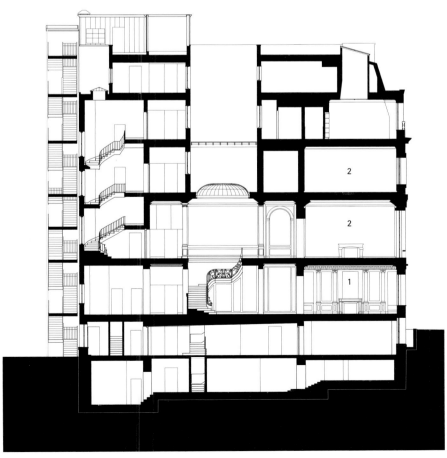

0   8'   16'   32'

Section Looking South

1   Café
2   Gallery

Neue Galerie, New York

Artists' Cabin

This cabin for two artists, located on a rocky promontory in a remote part of Nova Scotia, offers a private retreat defined by the landscape. The cabin is actually three separate structures: one for living and dining, one for sleeping, and the third for guests. Sited on a raised platform, the buildings' distributed arrangement establishes a series of distinct outdoor terraces with dramatic views.

The project's simple vocabulary is the result of the site's constraints: its isolated location and unpredictable weather required that all construction materials arrive by boat and be quickly assembled. Like the site's many granite boulders, the cabin appears as a gray figure in the landscape, clad with pale gray pine shingles and covered by single-sloped aluminum roofs. Inside, the project's wooden studs and sheathing remain exposed.

There is no electricity at the site; solar panels are the sole source of energy. The waterfront setting, unpopulated landscape, and quiet architecture make this a restorative seasonal retreat embodying the essence of shelter and simplicity.

Building Type: Residential
Construction Type: New Construction
Size: 900 sf (84 sm)

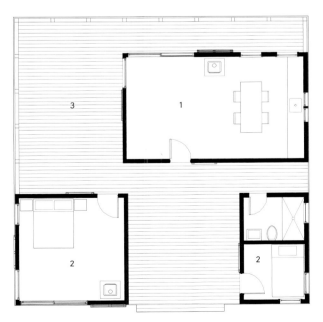

 0 2' 4'   8'

Floor Plan

1   Kitchen / Living Room / Dining Room
2   Bedroom
3   Deck

David Zwirner
19th Street

This Chelsea gallery occupies three single-story buildings originally conceived as horse stables and later used as auto-repair shops. The buildings were renovated sequentially. On the facade, large garage doors were replaced with storefront windows and doors, their configurations determined by the original openings. Inside, Selldorf Architects took cues from the proportions and arrangement of structural elements within each building to create an ensemble of diverse spaces united by a common architectural vocabulary. To the east the space was left with its original ceiling and accommodates new skylights. The other two buildings received a more comprehensive renovation, with new north-facing skylights throughout. Reveals where walls meet floors and slot registers where walls meet ceilings give the unadorned white surfaces crisp outlines.

Building Type: Cultural
Construction Type: Renovation
Size: 25,000 sf (2,323 sm)

```
⊘    0   6'   16'      32'
```

Ground-Floor Plan

1 Reception
2 Gallery
3 Office
4 Viewing Room
5 Art Storage
6 Prep
7 Deliveries
8 Storage / Prep

David Zwirner, 19th Street

Cologne Residence

Originally built in 1914, this estate in Cologne was renewed for modern living and stronger integration with the landscape. Selldorf Architects restored the historic architecture, simplifying exterior details and rebuilding the interior. The new 2,700-square-foot (251 square-meter) addition to the east is a striking modern design. Custom-carved tufa panels give the addition a handcrafted quality, creating resonance between the new architecture and the original brick-and-terra-cotta structure. The addition also brings a modern ethos to family living, with a new open and light-filled kitchen and dining area. Sliding glass enclosures allow the space to connect fully to new and refreshed outdoor areas, including a pool, a water feature, a dining terrace, and gardens. The rectilinearity of the new outdoor spaces is juxtaposed with the curved forms and Expressionist character of the surrounding gardens designed by Wirtz International. A new two-tiered mahogany-and-steel library on the second floor of the addition houses an extensive book collection. The modern detailing of the library is in sharp contrast to the historic expression of the original structure's interiors, but furnishings and accessories from Selldorf's custom line, Vica, unite the home's traditional and modern sensibilities.

Building Type: Residential
Construction Type: New Construction
and Renovation
Size: 27,000 sf (2,508 sm)
Executive Architect: Detlef Stephan Architekten

Cologne Residence

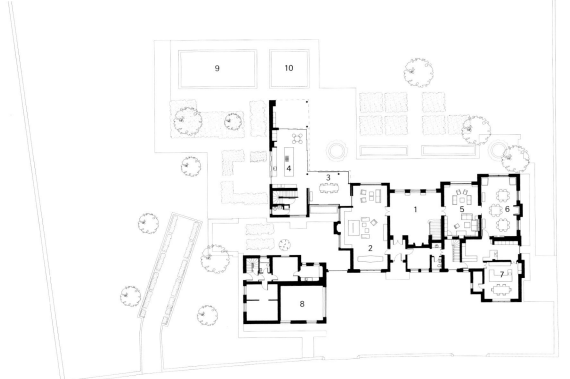

0   6'   16'   32'

Site Plan

1   Entry Foyer
2   Living Room
3   Family Dining Room
4   Kitchen
5   Salon
6   Formal Dining Room
7   Pantry
8   Guest House
9   Pool
10 Reflecting Pool

New York, NY, USA   2008

Gladstone Gallery 21st Street

Designed to house large sculpture and installation art, this new building located between Tenth and Eleventh Avenues in Chelsea, is a second exhibition space for the Gladstone Gallery. In acknowledgment of the industrial heritage of the neighborhood, the facade is made of dark gray extra-long Roman brick laid with filled joints to underscore the monumental appearance. The facade's large opening on the ground floor and ribbon windows on the upper levels reflect the functions within. The main exhibition space is a dramatic 50-square-foot (5-square-meter) column-free space with a 22-foot (7-meter) ceiling. The ceiling, with its exposed 36-inch-deep (91-centimeters-deep) trusses, is reminiscent of twentieth-century industrial studio space. The large single-sloped skylight—glazed with sandblasted wire glass—admits an abundance of daylight. A library on the main level and offices above complete the program.

Building Type: Cultural
Construction Type: New Construction
Size: 10,000 sf (929 sm)

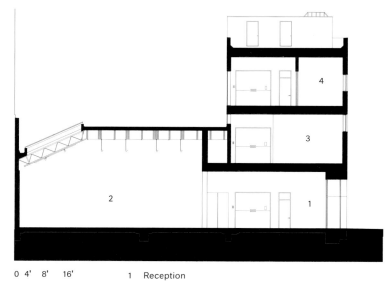

0 4' 8' 16'

Section Looking West

1 Reception
2 Gallery
3 Viewing Room
4 Office

0 4' 8' 16'

Ground-Floor Plan

1 Reception
2 Art Storage
3 Office
4 Gallery

144

Gladstone Gallery, 21st Street

Hauser & Wirth
69th Street

This new townhouse in a landmark district contains a gallery for contemporary art. The facade is composed of sandblasted cement stucco juxtaposed with limestone trim at the doors and windows. Tall windows and bronze railings accentuate the building's verticality. The large storefront windows at the ground level welcome passersby and open seamlessly to provide a loading entrance for large-scale works of art. The interior contains well proportioned flexible galleries. Daylight is provided via windows to the north and south and an open stair topped with a skylight.

Building Type: Cultural
Construction Type: New Construction
Size: 8,800 sf (818 sm)

Hauser & Wirth, 69th Street

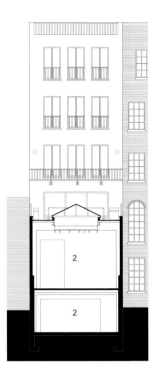

Section Looking North

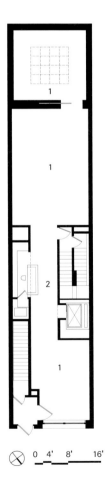

0 4' 8' 16'

Ground-Floor Plan

1 Gallery
2 Reception

Hauser & Wirth, 69th Street

Walden House

Located west of Vail, Colorado, within the White River National Forest mountain range at an elevation of 8,200 feet (2,499 meters), Walden house's main living spaces are oriented toward a new pond and take advantage of the spectacular views of the surrounding Gore Range and New York Mountains.

Designed as a series of smaller volumes arranged around a central courtyard, the enclosure creates an intimate counterpoint to the grandeur and scale of the surrounding mountain landscape. Internal circulation is organized along the perimeter of the courtyard, with the main living spaces opening directly from the corridor. The interpenetration of indoor and outdoor spaces fuses the architecture with its natural setting; the plantings and landscape design were done by Edwina Von Gal. Each volume has a distinct programmatic use and diverse material articulation. Local materials, including copper, field rock, log-pole siding, and stacked beetle-kill pine wood, reinforce the relationship between the building and its high mountain landscape.

Building Type: Residential
Construction Type: New Construction
Size: 12,000 sf (1,115 sm)

Walden House

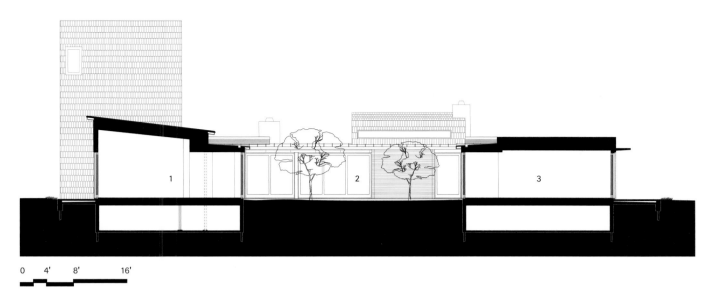

0 4' 8'   16'

Section Looking South

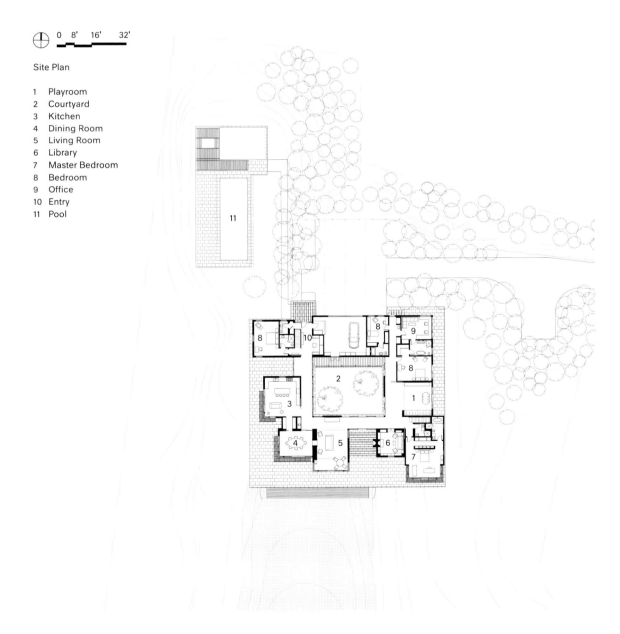

0 8' 16'   32'

Site Plan

1 Playroom
2 Courtyard
3 Kitchen
4 Dining Room
5 Living Room
6 Library
7 Master Bedroom
8 Bedroom
9 Office
10 Entry
11 Pool

London, UK   2010
Gagosian Gallery, Mayfair

Picasso: The Mediterranean Years (1945–1962)

Selldorf Architects has designed exhibitions for the Gagosian Gallery on several occasions, transforming its gallery spaces in New York and London. Distinct environments have been created for exhibitions of works by individual artists such as Pablo Picasso, Claude Monet, Robert Rauschenberg, and Lucio Fontana, among others. For each exhibition, Selldorf Architects developed a layout and lighting design appropriate for the specific artist's work.

The design of *Picasso: The Mediterranean Years (1945–1962)* at Gagosian's Britannia Street gallery in London was a complex undertaking. It required a reconfiguration of the space from five to seven rooms to accommodate a diverse range of work, from large sculpture to paintings. In addition, Selldorf Architects designed the vitrines and pedestals for the display of freestanding works.

Building Type: Exhibition Design
Size: 9,400 sf (873 sm)

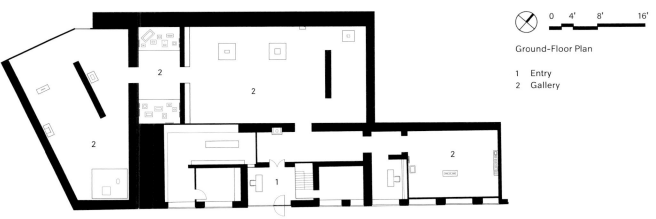

0   4'   8'   16'

Ground-Floor Plan

1   Entry
2   Gallery

Picasso: The Mediterranean Years

Hauser & Wirth
Savile Row

Hauser & Wirth's gallery on London's Savile Row is composed of two distinct column-free exhibition spaces and a separate level for private showrooms and administrative functions. The main exhibition spaces are distinguished in character and feel by their contrasting scales and material palettes. The north gallery's soaring proportions and concrete floors are suited to the display of large sculpture, whereas the south gallery's more intimate scale is expressed with wood flooring and laylight. Both spaces offer the calm and focus essential for the contemplation of works by modern and contemporary masters. A library, offices, and viewing rooms are located on the second floor.

Building Type: Cultural
Construction Type: Renovation
Size: 20,000 sf (1,858 sm)
Executive Architects: Eric Parry Architects and Ben Adams Architects

Hauser & Wirth, Savile Row

200 Eleventh Avenue

This residential building is located in New York's West Chelsea neighborhood, a former industrial zone, and home to many art galleries. The building makes an iconic contribution to the neighborhood while establishing continuity with Chelsea's architectural traditions. Located at a busy corner with vehicular and pedestrian traffic, the building needed to relate at both scales. The base anchors the building to its surroundings by reflecting the low-rise scale of the neighborhood and through a material palette (terra-cotta cladding and blackened-steel window frames) that evokes the masonry facades and details of industrial Chelsea. Above the plinth, the tower energizes the neighborhood with a new architectural expression: the metallic sheen and organic form of its custom-fabricated stainless steel rainscreen.

The sixteen units are configured as duplexes—a strategy that increases building height in order to maximize river views. Each unit has the feel of a private home, with a double-height living space. The innovative design of a car elevator on the east facade of the building allows for an individual garage space on each floor, providing a high level of privacy for the owners. Interiors are modern and flexible— the kitchens can be fluidly integrated with the living area or concealed by teak folding doors that, when closed, reveal themselves as wood-paneled walls. All apartments are afforded open views of the Hudson River that are maximized by full-height casement windows.

Building Type: Residential
Construction Type: New Construction
Size: 60,000 sf (5,574 sm)
Executive Architect: Steven Kratchman Architect

200 Eleventh Avenue

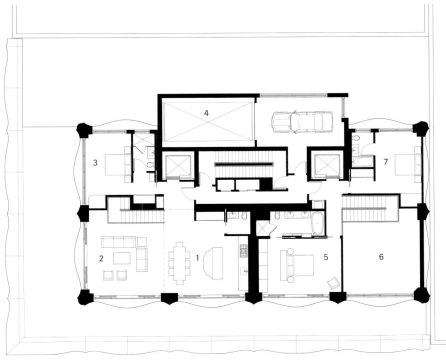

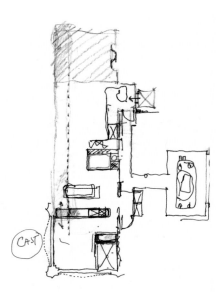

0 4' 8' 16'

Lower Level of North Unit

1 Kitchen and Dining Room
2 Living Room
3 Bedroom
4 Car Elevator

Upper Level of South Unit

5 Master Bedroom
6 Open to Living Room Below
7 Bedroom

VeneKlasen Carriage House

This residence is located along a historic street in Greenwich Village that originally served as a private carriageway for houses on Washington Square. The mews has been home to artists Isamu Noguchi, Jackson Pollock, and Gertrude Vanderbilt Whitney.

The main floor contains a gracious, double-height living room that receives abundant daylight through its ten-foot-tall, south-facing windows and an open stair which connects all levels of the house. A focal point of this room is an eighteenth-century gilt wood-and-zinc Karl Friedrich Schinkel chandelier.

The entry level includes a dining room and kitchen with access to the garden patio. A glass entry vestibule was added to define space in the otherwise open layout. The master bedroom is located on the upper floor, adjacent to a new roof garden terrace. Interior design harmoniously incorporates Selldorf's custom Vica furniture with the client's period and modern furnishings and eclectic collection of paintings, drawings, and objects.

Building Type: Residential
Construction Type: Renovation
Size: 1,920 sf (178 sm)

VeneKlasen Carriage House

The Mesa at Amangiri

The Mesa at Amangiri, a planned collection of thirty-six villas, is located in a spectacular high-desert setting with access to the services and amenities of the adjacent Amangiri resort. The modern designs are integrated with the surrounding landscape through their low-rise scale and the use of materials, colors, and textures that complement the site and the resort. The villas, each with a shaded arrival court, are organized around dramatic masonry walls that define a series of airy, interconnected spaces. The design creates seamless transitions between the indoors and outdoors: living and dining spaces open completely to a large pool terrace and wide expansive vistas, and the bedroom suites open to private garden terraces and more intimate views. Buildings and paved roads have been sited to reduce the effect on fragile desert flora, and energy use is moderated through the orientation of buildings, brise-soleils for shading, geothermal heating and cooling, and localized solar water heating.

Building Type: Residential
Construction Type: New Construction
Size: 250-acre (101-hectare) Site; Individual Mesas Range: 10,000–16,200 sf (929–1,505 sm)

The Mesa at Amangiri

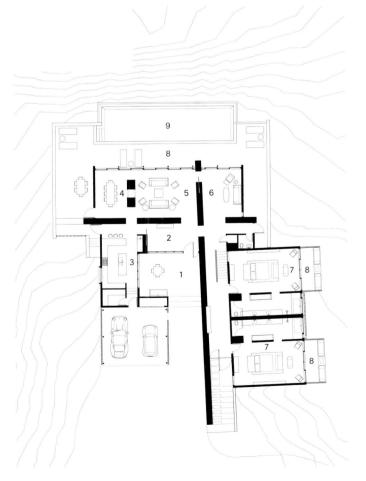

0 4' 8' 16'

Site Plan

1 Entry
2 Foyer
3 Kitchen
4 Dining Room
5 Living Room
6 Media Room
7 Bedroom
8 Terrace
9 Pool

The Mesa at Amangiri

Le Stanze del Vetro

Le Stanze del Vetro is a museum dedicated to twentieth- and twenty-first-century glassmaking founded by Pentagram Stiftung and supported by Fondazione Giorgio Cini. Located on the island of San Giorgio Maggiore in Venice, the museum is part of a campus of historic buildings that have been restored and repurposed for cultural and educational uses. The museum hosts exhibitions and events highlighting artists who use glass as an original means of expression.

Housed on the ground floor of a former boarding school, the museum retains the school's rationalist vocabulary and interior configuration. The design transforms existing classrooms into seven intimately scaled galleries for temporary exhibitions and connects them with a new enfilade passageway. Windows along the perimeter bring controlled natural light into the galleries. Vitrines mounted inside the original classroom doorways create a visually permeable separation between the corridor and individual galleries. Sculptural Murano glass ceiling fixtures were designed by artist Alessandro Diaz de Santillana, who designed the steel shelving in the bookshop and along the original corridor. The shelving was based on an original design by his father Ludovico Diaz de Santillana, son of Paulo Venini.

Other functional requirements are incorporated into the design, including a new accessible entrance, a reception area, a bookshop, a media room, restrooms, and storage. In keeping with Venice's tradition of craftsmanship, the firm worked closely with local artisans—notably, Carlo Capovilla, Francesco Zanon, and Maurizio Torcellan—on the design of the museum's custom Italian walnut-and-steel vitrines.

Building Type: Cultural
Construction Type: Renovation
Size: 7,800 sf (725 sm)

Le Stanze del Vetro

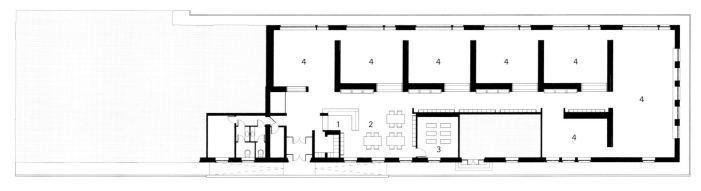

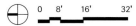

0   8'   16'   32'

Ground-Floor Plan

1   Reception
2   Book Shop
3   Media
4   Gallery

Le Stanze del Vetro

David Zwirner London

Located in Mayfair, London's historic fine-arts district, this eighteenth-century Georgian townhouse was transformed into David Zwirner's first gallery in Europe. The building has a rich history; once the private residence of a British prime minister, it was later transformed into a spa owned by Helena Rubinstein, and most recently housed a private bank. Several centuries of renovations resulted in the need for extensive work to create new spaces with the proportions, lighting, and mechanical systems essential to the display of contemporary art. The design utilizes the Minimalist sensibility that Selldorf Architects created for David Zwirner's New York galleries, adapting it for the domestic scale of a townhouse, with oak flooring and window scrims that modulate natural light. The gallery contains three levels of public exhibition spaces; offices, private showrooms, and a library are located on the two levels above.

Building Type: Cultural
Construction Type: Renovation
Size: 10,000 sf (929 sm)
Executive Architect: Cowie Montgomery Architects

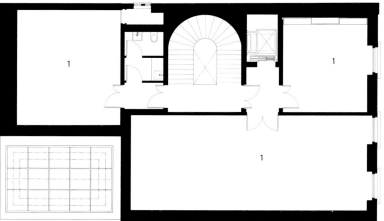

0 2' 4' 8'

Typical Upper-Floor Plan

1   Gallery

David Zwirner, London

Van de Weghe Townhouse

This 1887 townhouse, located in a landmarked district on Manhattan's Upper East Side, was completely transformed; only the historic front facade remains of the original house. To increase the ceiling heights throughout, the garden level was lowered by 3 feet (1 meter), which also created a seamless transition from interior to exterior space, and the rear roof was raised, resulting in gracious ceiling heights at the upper level. Light permeates the building: an oval skylight brings natural light down through the five levels of the house; and the new rear facade, with full-height glass windows, maximizes light and transparency. The interior detailing and finishes are respectful of the townhouse typology, yet expressed in a modern vocabulary.

Building Type: Residential
Construction Type: New Construction and Renovation
Size: 8,400 sf (780 sm)

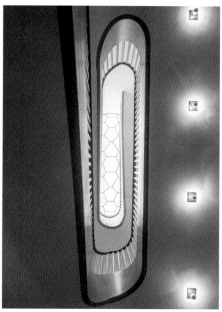

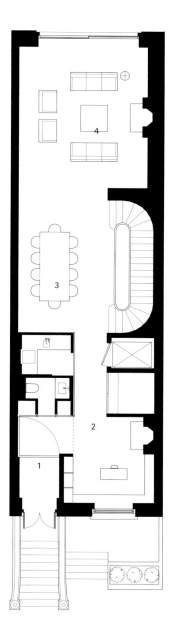

Second-Floor Plan

1 Entry
2 Office
3 Dining Room
4 Living Room

Van de Weghe Residence

Hauser & Wirth
18th Street

The Roxy, a former roller rink and nightclub, was transformed into Hauser & Wirth's second gallery in New York—a vast column-free space dedicated to the display of large-scale contemporary art. The gallery has a unique circulation sequence that draws visitors up a long, sweeping stairway before revealing the main exhibition space: a single 10,000-square-foot (929-square-meter) gallery. Inside the space, the existing wood ceilings were restored, large steel trusses were refinished, and skylights were uncovered and enlarged. Three smaller galleries complement the main exhibition space and private showrooms; a library and offices provide additional program space. Several artists contributed to the project, including Björn Roth, who designed the gallery's Roth Bar as a tribute to his father, Dieter Roth; and Martin Creed, who created a custom installation for the entrance-stair hall.

Building Type: Cultural
Construction Type: Renovation
Size: 24,700 sf (2,295 sm)

Main-Level Plan

1   Entry
2   Reception
3   Gallery
4   Viewing Room
5   Workshop / Art Storage
6   Office / Library / Conference
7   Roth Bar

West Village Residence

This new mixed-use building is located in the West Village, a landmarked neighborhood with intimate blocks composed of townhomes, low-rise multifamily buildings, and vestiges of its warehouse past. Creating a balance between forward-looking new architecture and neighborhood continuity informed the generative concept. The design's controlled modern volumes bring strong definition to the corner site, yet are also compatible with the surrounding townhouses' simple, linear forms. Handcrafted red Roman brick on the street facade and luminous off-white terra-cotta on the garden side, both with blackened-steel window frames, demonstrate a contextual sensibility that is expressed within a new contemporary framework.

The building contains commercial office and retail space on the ground level and a two-story private residence above, set back from the base. A large elevated courtyard on the west side of the building serves as a private outdoor garden for the residents. Rooms are organized around the perimeter of the courtyard, creating views from almost every space in the home. Terraces on the upper levels extend the outdoor atmosphere throughout the residence. The simple program includes large and light-filled living spaces with a private glass-enclosed rooftop study with impressive views. Horticulturalist Piet Oudolf designed the garden and roof terrace plantings.

Building Type: Cultural
Construction Type: New Construction
Size: 25,000 sf (2,323 sm)

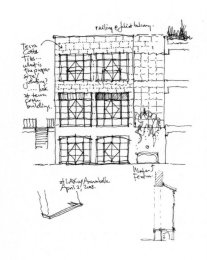

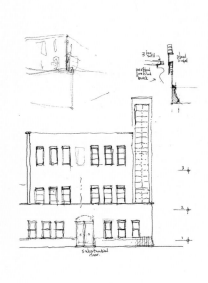

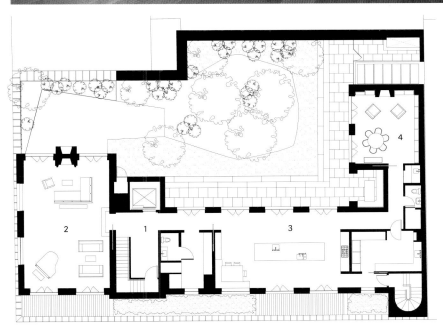

0 4' 8' 16'

Main-Level Plan

1   Entry
2   Living Room
3   Kichen
4   Library

David Zwirner 20th Street

West Chelsea's industrial heritage inspired the simple monumentality of this ground-up gallery building. Made from exposed board-formed concrete, the facade is both rough and refined—having the grittiness to resonate with neighboring structures and the elegance to create a distinguished identity for the gallery. The teak storefront creates a warm contrast with the concrete and allows the building to open for art loading.

The gallery is built to museum standards and was specifically designed to accommodate the range of artists the gallery represents—including modern masters such as Dan Flavin and Donald Judd. Gallery spaces are diverse in scale, materiality, and lighting, offering a flexible range of environments for art. The main exhibition space is an expansive 5,000-square-foot (1,525-square-meter) column-free gallery with concrete floors and four north-facing sawtooth skylights. Public exhibition space continues on the second floor with a more intimate series of galleries expressed with oak flooring and vertical light. The upper levels contain viewing rooms, offices, a library, and art-handling areas.

A five-story central open stair, topped with a skylight, creates a counterpoint to the restrained exhibition spaces. The exposed concrete of the facade continues through the entry to the atrium stair walls. The first LEED-certified commercial gallery in the United States, this LEED Gold project incorporates five green roof spaces—with plantings designed by Piet Oudolf—premium-efficiency mechanicals, maximized daylighting, and locally and responsibly sourced materials.

Building Type: Cultural
Construction Type: New Construction
Size: 30,000 sf (2,787 sm)

David Zwirner, 20th Street

David Zwirner, 20th Street

David Zwirner, 20th Street

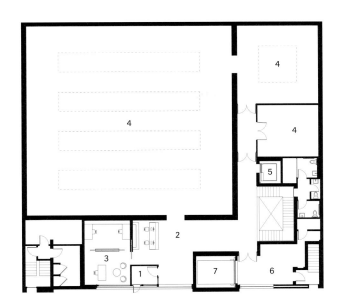

Ground-Floor Plan

1   Entry
2   Reception
3   Office
4   Gallery
5   Passenger Elevator
6   Art Handling
7   Freight Elevator
8   Green Roof
9   Viewing Room

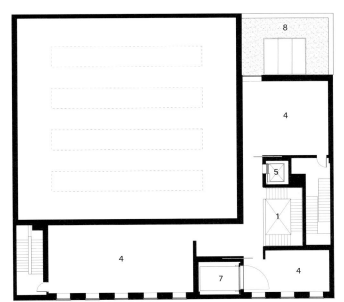

Second-Floor Plan

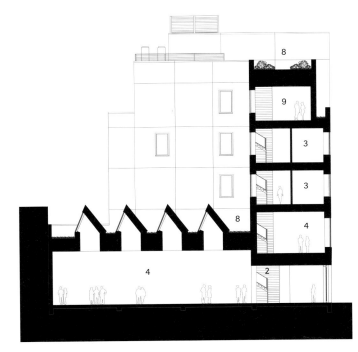

Section Looking East

David Zwirner, 20th Street

The Encyclopedic Palace

For the 2013 Venice Biennale, Annabelle Selldorf collaborated with curator Massimiliano Gioni on the architectural layout for the central exhibition, *The Encyclopedic Palace*. The exhibition was presented in the Arsenale, a vast complex of former shipyards and armories.

The design transformed the long, linear space of the Arsenale into a cohesive series of galleries suited to contemporary art. One of the most significant architectural interventions ever undertaken in the space, the design covered most of the historic brick walls with new white surfaces and subdivided the at times overwhelming spaces of the complex into more intimate rooms. The plan subverted the existing linear circulation with diverse configurations that encouraged visitors to slowly wind their way through the exhibition. Lighting the immense windowless space was achieved by covering the dark central ceiling arcade with a white fabric scrim and distributing artificial lighting evenly across the space.

Building Type: Exhibition Design
Size: 69,000 sf (6,410 sm)

The Encyclopedic Palace

Brooklyn, NY, USA   2013
Sims Municipal Recycling

Sunset Park Material Recovery Facility

The Sunset Park Material Recovery Facility is a processing center for New York City's curbside metal, glass, and plastic recyclables undertaken by Sims Municipal Recycling and the City of New York. Located on an 11-acre (4.5-hectare) waterfront pier, the design's programmatic use as a recycling center inspired reuse throughout.

The master plan arranges buildings to support functionality, creates distinct circulation systems to separate visitors from operations, and adds 2 acres (1 hectare) of native plantings. Buildings are organized to create the site's own urban context. The facility includes a tipping building, where recyclables arrive by barge and truck; processing and bale-storage buildings; and an administrative and education center. The education center houses programs for students and the public, and includes classrooms, exhibitions, and interactive demonstration displays. A pedestrian bridge connects the education center to a viewing platform inside the processing facility, providing an opportunity to watch the recycling process firsthand.

One of the design challenges in working with a pre-engineered building was to find ways to articulate the program and give an overall expression to the facility. In response, structural elements are inverted to appear on the exterior, giving steel girders and lateral bracing a greater visual impact.

Recycled materials are used throughout: site fill is made from a composite of recycled glass, asphalt, and rock reclaimed from the city's Second Avenue Line subway construction; buildings are made from recycled steel; and plazas are finished with recycled glass. Other sustainable measures include one of the largest applications of photovoltaics in New York, a wind turbine, and bioswales for storm-water management.

Building Type: Commercial
Construction Type: New Construction
Size: 140,000 sf (13,006 sm)

Sunset Park Material Recovery Facility

Sunset Park Material Recovery Facility

Sunset Park Material Recovery Facility

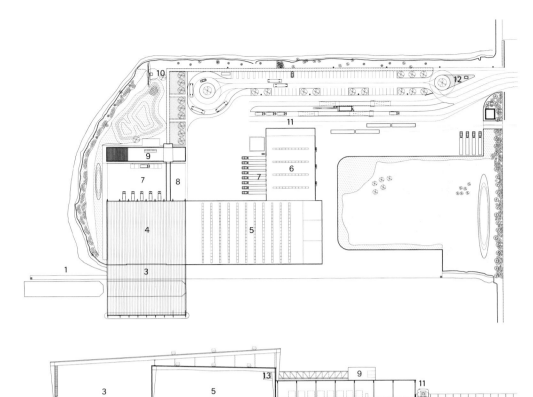
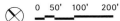

Section Looking West

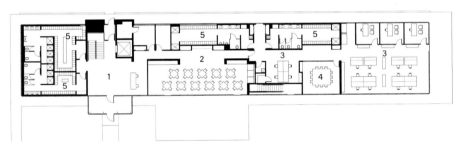

Ground-Floor Plan

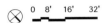

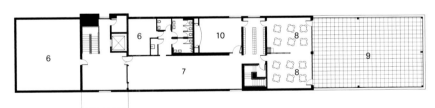

Second-Floor Plan

Third-Floor Plan

Chelsea Townhouse

This four-story townhouse in the Chelsea Historic District received a full renovation, including a new rear facade and extension.

An existing 12-foot- (4-meter-) deep, one-story addition in the rear garden was removed and replaced by a new extension that encompasses all of the floors. Full-height casement windows maximize the south-facing light while preserving the intimate scale of the house. New balconies were added at each upper floor, creating a deeper connection between the house and the garden.

The interior is organized around a dramatic sculptural skylit staircase. Its sinuous curvature links the floors together and creates a counterpoint to the rectilinearity of the basic townhouse footprint. A limited palette of finish materials, including white oak flooring, Venetian plaster walls, and a blackened-metal stair rail that matches the hearths of the home's two fireplaces, contribute to a general sense of calm and focus.

Building Type: Residential
Construction Type: New Construction and Renovation
Size: 5,600 sf (520 sm)

Chelsea Townhouse

1000 Dean Street and Berg'n

1000 Dean Street and Berg'n are significant catalysts for regeneration in the Crown Heights neighborhood of Brooklyn. The project revives a dilapidated former Studebaker Service Station and adjacent brick garage, transforming two remnants of Brooklyn's industrial heritage into a new community destination. Restored architecture is invigorated by new functions, including a food hall–style restaurant, indoor market, and creative office studios—programs that enliven the neighborhood with commercial activity and new amenities.

1000 Dean Street's vast floor plates and industrial character create an ideal setting for the winter home of Brooklyn Flea, a renowned market specializing in local food, crafts, and vintage wares. Attracting thousands of visitors each weekend, the market establishes the project as a major New York City destination. Above the market, the building's upper floors contain light-filled studio and office space for Brooklyn's creative and tech companies as well as nonprofits. The renovation maintains the building's raw, open quality but updates it for contemporary uses with a new circulation core, two expansive light wells, and modern building systems.

Located in the adjacent brick garage, Berg'n is a food hall–style restaurant and coffee bar where visitors can enjoy casual food made by local vendors. The space's open floor plan, courtyard, and picnic table–style seating encourage interaction and a feeling of community. A mix of vintage and modern finishes, fixtures, and furnishings work together to create a contemporary design that evokes the building's industrial past.

Building Type: Commercial
Construction Type: Renovation
Size: 164,000 sf (15,236 sm)
Executive Architect for Berg'n: Bostudio Architecture

1000 Dean Street and Berg'n

Brown University John Hay Library

Built in 1910 by Shepley, Rutan, and Coolidge, the John Hay Library was Brown University's first dedicated library building. In the century that followed, numerous renovations occurred, along with the conversion of the building into a library for special collections. The grandeur and function of the original Reading Room were lost with the subdivision of the space into three distinct rooms for collections handling and administration.

Selldorf Architects' main objective in the renovation was to return a vital part of Brown's heritage to the campus through a design that restores key elements of the original library, but also responds to the needs of a contemporary university. The design reestablishes the original proportions of the Reading Room, restores oak shelving displays, and introduces replicas of the library's original pendant lighting. New furnishings, including tables and lounge seating, recall the original design, but provide a more flexible range of environments for study with diverse configurations. State-of-the-art technology-infrastructure upgrades support the university's twenty-first-century needs without compromising its historic character.

The new design clarifies the once confusing circulation on the main level and welcomes visitors with a more gracious entry sequence. New glass doors and inset wall vitrines create a transparent and communicative interface between the entry vestibule and the Reading Room. Selldorf Architects designed other key public spaces, including Reader Services, the Special Collections Reading Room, a gallery, a conference room, and a study café.

Building Type: Institutional
Construction Type: Renovation
Size: 80,000 sf (7,432 sm)

Brown University, John Hay Library

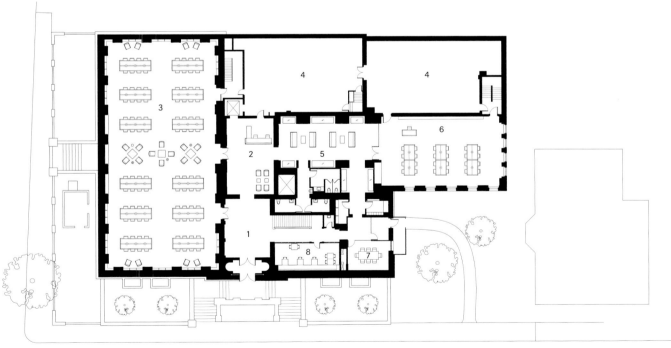

0 8' 16' 32'	1 Entry
	2 Reader Services
Main-Level Plan	3 Main Reading Room
	4 Stacks
	5 Gallery Lounge
	6 Special Collections Reading Room
	7 Conference Room
	8 Café

Brown University, John Hay Library

Skarstedt Residence

Located a short walk from the ocean, this summer retreat for an art-collecting couple and their family is defined by a series of taut mahogany volumes. An entry court is formed by two symmetrical one-story volumes off of the main two-story bar building. Inside, a triple-height atrium stair provides open views directly to the garden. The home's public spaces—the living room, dining room, and kitchen—are organized along the south facade with sliding glass walls that open fully to the pool and gardens, which were designed by Miranda Brooks. The seamless transition between indoor and outdoor living is further enhanced by the shade-giving steel trellis with fabric canopy and mahogany brise-soleils.

The central stair brings filtered daylight and natural breezes into the home with operable windows and mahogany louvers. The upper level comprises a master suite, a den, and four bedrooms, with a rooftop terrace providing panoramic views.

Building Type: Residential
Construction Type: New Construction
Size: 10,000 sf (929 sm)

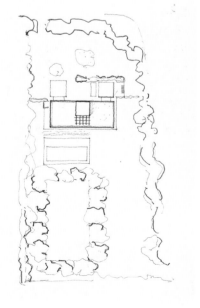

Skarstedt Residence

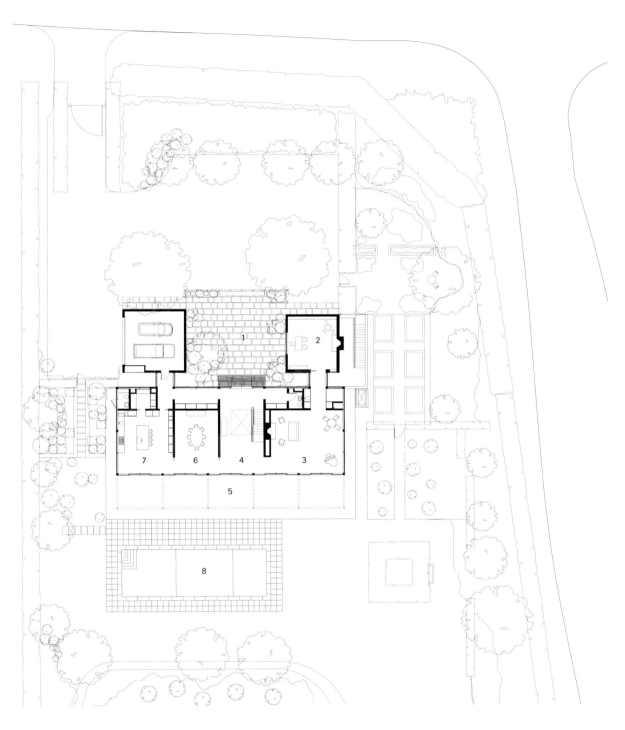

0 12'   24'   48'

Site Plan

1 Courtyard
2 Study
3 Living Room
4 Entry Foyer
5 Terrace
6 Dining Room
7 Kitchen
8 Pool

Williamstown, MA, USA
2014 (Museum)
2016 (Manton Research Center)

Clark Art Institute

The Clark is an art museum and research center located on a 140-acre (56-hectare) campus in the Berkshires. As part of a major expansion project, Selldorf Architects, working with Gensler as executive architect, was commissioned to design the renovation of the original Museum Building and the Manton Research Center.

The museum, built in 1955 by Daniel Perry, houses the Clark's permanent collection of European and American paintings, sculpture, and decorative arts. The renovation restores and enhances the building's distinct character while also bringing it into the twenty-first century. The Clark's overall expansion included a reorganization of the campus orientation and a new building serving as the main visitor entry. This resulted in a reconfigured circulation for the museum, with entry now being possible on the west end of the building and the conversion of former back-of-house space into galleries. Creating a new rhythm in the corridors and galleries enhances the art-viewing experience and enables increased focus by visitors. Throughout the building, original details were simplified, and new, state-of-the-art mechanical and lighting systems introduced, resulting in a calmer and more welcoming environment overall.

The Manton Research Center was designed in 1973 by Pietro Belluschi and the Architects' Collaborative to house the Clark's art library, administrative and scholar offices, and an auditorium. The renovation enhances research facilities and welcomes the public by recasting the former visitor services area into a new public Reading Room. The Reading Room is a central, light-filled gathering space where scholars, museum staff, and the public come together. The new Study Center for Works on Paper provides students and scholars with access to the Clark's collection of rare books and prints.

Building Type: Cultural
Construction Type: Renovation
Size: 150,000 sf (13,935 sm)
Executive Architect: Gensler

Clark Art Institute

Clark Art Institute

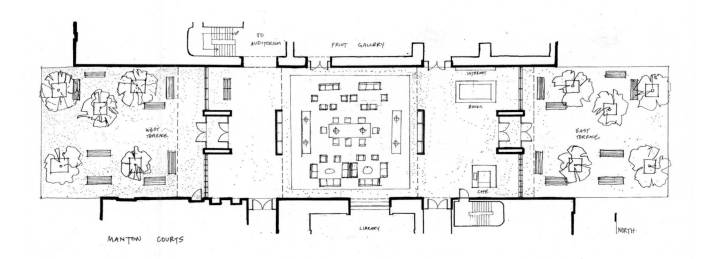

0 8' 16' 32'

Ground-Floor Plan

1 Entrance Court
2 Reading Room
3 Coffee Bar / Book Store
4 Library
5 Director's Suite
6 Gallery
7 Study Center for Works on Paper
8 Auditorium
9 Connection to Museum

Martha Washington and Marta

The Martha Washington, Manhattan's iconic hotel for women, which opened in 1903, has been revived and reimagined for a contemporary audience. Selldorf Architects restored portions of the building's landmarked facade and designed key public spaces, including the restaurant and lounge—amenities that make the hotel a vibrant neighborhood destination. The entire first-floor slab was demolished and rebuilt 3 feet (1 meter) lower, making it continuous with the sidewalk. Window openings were elongated and replaced with operable glass doors at the street, which enhance visibility and connectivity.

The hotel welcomes the public with Marta, a Roman-style restaurant. Two large tiled pizza ovens are the focal point of the dining room, fronted by a pizza bar where guests can observe the chefs at work. Tall ceilings recall the grand proportions of turn-of-the-twentieth-century architecture, whereas the interiors are decidedly modern. A controlled palette of common design elements, including blue cement-tile floors, white fluted columns, and walnut millwork, bring continuity to the diverse public spaces. Furnishings and fixtures are custom-designed by Selldorf Architects—everything from the velvet banquettes to the smoked-glass rod pendants.

Building Type: Commercial
Construction Type: Renovation
Size: 30,000 sf (2,787 sm)

Martha Washington and Marta

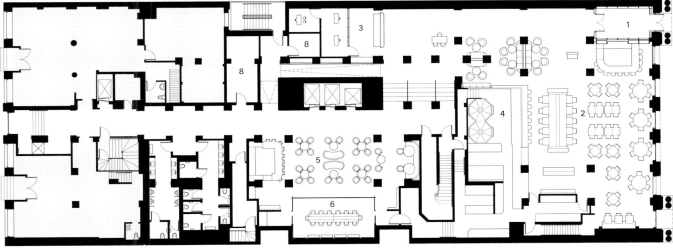

0   16'   32'   64'

Main-Level Plan

1   Entry
2   Restaurant
3   Hotel Reception
4   Open Kitchen
5   Hotel Bar
6   Private Dining Room

Luma Arles

Luma Arles is a new contemporary art center that brings together artists, researchers, and creators from every field to collaborate on multidisciplinary works and exhibitions. Located south of Arles's historic city center, the project repurposes the industrial ruins of a 16-acre (6.5-hectare) rail depot and introduces a new park for the public. Selldorf Architects is part of a team of designers, including Frank Gehry and Bas Smets, working on the complex. In addition to contributing to the overall master plan, Selldorf Architects is designing the renovation and conversion of two former rail structures into new exhibition facilities.

The project balances nineteenth-century industrial vocabulary with the art center's contemporary purpose. The original structures were maintained while creating a rhythm of indoor and outdoor spaces. Steel columns and trusses were refinished and skylights relocated and expanded, in service of creating flexible, well-proportioned spaces with natural light and clear circulation.

A new open-air courtyard includes a café and serves as a communal gathering space for presentations and concerts. Les Forges (2014), the original foundry building, contains two levels of gallery space totaling 31,500 square feet (2,926 square meters). The restored Mécanique Générale (2016) is a 48,000-square-foot (4,459-square-meter) structure containing exhibition space and artist workshops. A new bay creates a 65-foot (20-meter) column-free span in the historic space. The modern addition's exposed steel frame, concrete facade, and zinc roof create a resonant contrast with the existing structure.

Building Type: Cultural
Construction Type: New Construction and Renovation
Size: 79,500 sf (7,386 sm)
Executive Architect: C+D Architecture

Luma Arles

Luma Arles

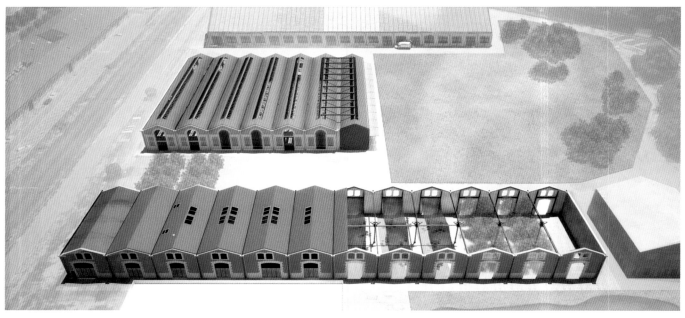

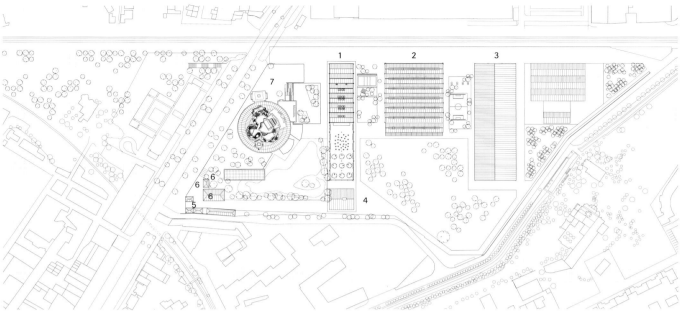

0 64' 128' 256'

1   Les Forges—Exhibition
2   La Mécanique Général—Exhibition
3   La Grande Halle—Multi-Purpose
4   La Formation—Dance Studio and Artists' Residence
5   La Maison du Projet—Café and Visitor Center
6   Centre Médico-Social—Hotel
7   Art and Research Center

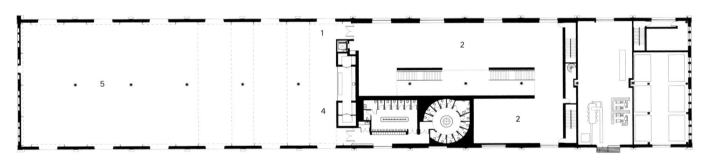

Les Forges

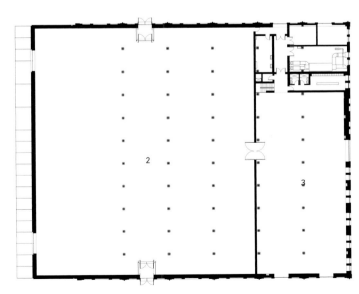

La Mécanique Général

0 16' 32' 64'

Ground-Floor Plan

1   Entry
2   Gallery
3   Workshop
4   Café / Bar
5   Courtyard

House in the Springs

Located on a quiet beachfront site in the Springs, this family retreat is composed of a pair of homes. The two residences and a connecting breezeway frame a central garden with lush plantings, covered terraces, and a pool. Together they create a cohesive ensemble of indoor and outdoor living spaces where family and guests can gather to enjoy spectacular views of Gardiners Bay. The simple volumes echo local architectural traditions with cedar shingles, sloped roofs, and punched window openings, yet their overall impact is confidently modern. Cedar shingles are complemented by rich mahogany pergolas that envelop and connect the two homes, reinforcing the relationship between the buildings while also creating shaded outdoor areas and balconies, as well as framing diverse coastal and garden views. Abby Clough Lawless was the landscape architect.

To the east, the main residence is composed of three smaller volumes that create differentiated areas for entertaining on the ground floor. On the upper level, a master suite and two bedrooms have direct ocean views, whereas a playroom and study overlook a garden. Across the courtyard, the guest residence and pool terrace create a balanced dialogue with the main house. The guesthouse has an open kitchen and living space, with three bedrooms on the level above.

Building Type: Residential
Construction Type: New Construction
Size: 10,500 sf (975 sm)

House in the Springs

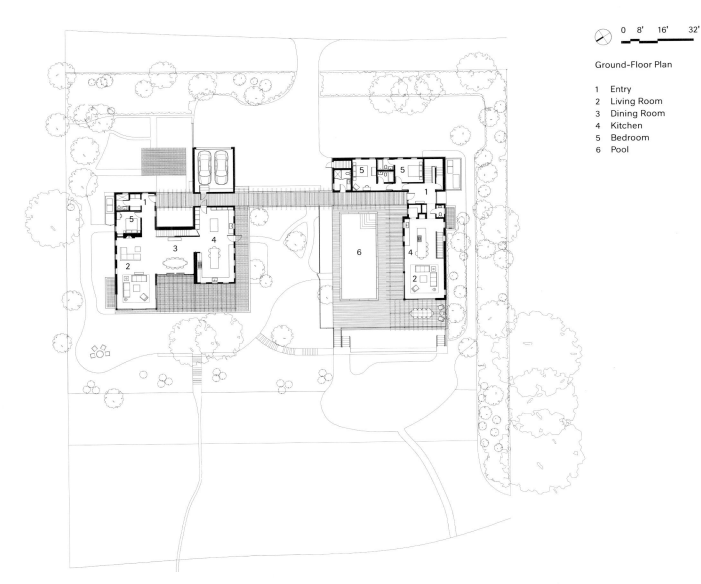

0   8'   16'   32'

Ground-Floor Plan

1   Entry
2   Living Room
3   Dining Room
4   Kitchen
5   Bedroom
6   Pool

House in the Springs

10 Bond Street

This new residential building makes a strong contribution to New York's NoHo neighborhood, a landmarked district characterized by elegant loft structures built during the late-nineteenth and early-twentieth centuries. The modern design resonates with the surrounding historic buildings by echoing their low-rise scale, regular rhythm of structural bays, large windows, and highly crafted facades. Terra-cotta, a material traditionally used to create architectural ornament, forms 10 Bond Street's distinctive exterior. Individual terra-cotta panels are custom-cast with a curved profile, glazed in a deep russet reminiscent of the area's brick neighbors, and trimmed with weathered steel. Inside, the seven-story building contains a maisonette, nine private apartments with open loftlike layouts, and a penthouse with a brise-soleil-covered terrace and roof garden. Expansive glass windows provide urban views, immersing each unit in natural light and its surrounding architectural context. Retail shops on the ground level facing the busier Lafayette Street welcome the public and link the building programmatically to the neighborhood.

Building Type: Residential
Construction Type: New Construction
Size: 34,000 sf (3,159 sm)

10 Bond Street

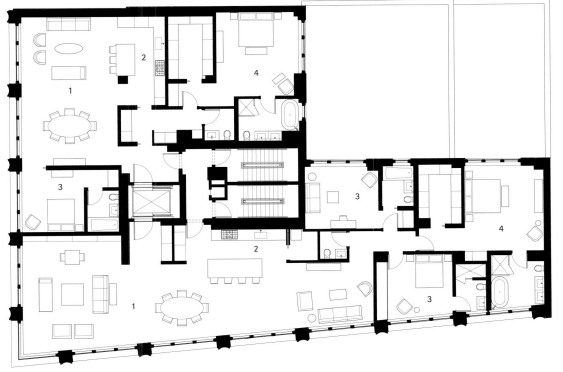

Typical Floor Plan

1 Living / Dining Room
2 Kitchen
3 Bedroom
4 Master Bedroom

42 Crosby Street

42 Crosby Street evokes the essential qualities of SoHo's cast-iron buildings—their uniform composition, column-and-spandrel vocabulary, and use of prefabricated construction techniques—articulating them through a strong modern design. Stainless steel, brushed aluminum, metal mesh, and exterior shades, are layered to create the depth, texture, and play of shadow and light that characterize the neighborhood's historic architecture. The resulting architecture resonates with its context, yet is also something new and transcendent. Presenting a strong corner presence, the residential building contains nine private apartments and a penthouse, with retail shops at the ground level and parking below.

Building Type: Residential
Construction Type: New Construction
Size: 50,000 sf (4,645 sm)
Executive Architect: Union Street Studio

42 Crosby Street

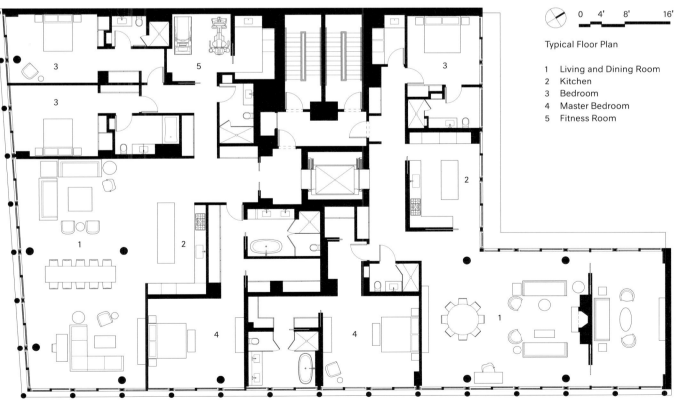

Typical Floor Plan

1   Living and Dining Room
2   Kitchen
3   Bedroom
4   Master Bedroom
5   Fitness Room

0   4'   8'   16'

Steinway & Sons Steinway Hall

Steinway & Sons was founded in New York City in 1853, and the company has been manufacturing and showcasing pianos in the city ever since. It has a rich architectural history, from its large factory in Astoria, Queens, to the Steinway Building on West 57th Street. The newest Steinway Hall is prominently located in the base of a modern limestone-and-steel high-rise in midtown on Avenue of the Americas. Affectionately known as the "center of the piano universe," Steinway Hall welcomes music lovers of all types, from passionate listeners to professional artists.

Inspired by Steinway's legacy of craftsmanship at the highest level, Selldorf Architects' design creates a strong contemporary presence for the legendary piano maker. Steinway Hall welcomes the public to a large, light-filled showroom with expansive windows at the busy pedestrian street level. Refined details like oak-end grain floors and a custom bentwood ceiling bring craft and character to the modern space, linking it with the company's history.

A focal point of the design is a central open stair that connects the showroom to the level below. Artist Spencer Finch has created a hanging-light installation inspired by Johann Sebastian Bach's Goldberg Variations through the stairwell. The lower level includes a recital hall, recording studio, and concert-artist space. The seventy-two-seat recital hall is an intimate performance venue for public concerts and private recording sessions. The hall's tilted wood-veneer panels create superb acoustics and bring a sense of warmth and scale to the recital space.

Building Type: Cultural
Construction Type: Renovation
Size: 17,500 sf (1,626 sm)

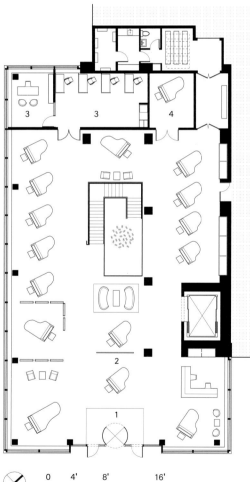

0   4'   8'   16'

Main-Level Plan

1   Entry
2   Piano Showroom
3   Office
4   Practice Room

Steinway & Sons, Steinway Hall

Martha's Vineyard Residence

This compound restores the character of the site to its agrarian roots. The 7-acre (2.8-hectare) site was first populated in the early 1800s with a small saltbox cottage and added to over time with a second, smaller cabin to the north and a large barn. The cottage is being restored to its 1850 size, and the barn, which was demolished during a hurricane in the 1940s, is being rebuilt according to historic records and will be used as a studio. A new single-story glass house will serve as the main living space for the family.

The buildings of historic descent are clustered together on the northwest corner of the site, creating an almost village-like setting. The new house is situated across an open lawn to the east abutting a very large meadow and acting as a bridge between the more cultivated and natural parts of the property.

Sited on a stone platform lightly depressed into the landscape, the house is a simple rectangle comprised of floor-to-ceiling, 5 x 12-foot (1.5 x 3.7-meter) fixed and operable glazing units. The structure is made of wood, with slender cedar columns placed outside of the glazing, allowing for column-free space in the interior. The layout of the living spaces is designed to coincide with the modular window units and provides for circulation along the perimeter. The roof is placed so as to minimize heat gain with a larger overhang over a terrace to the south and west exposures. Shade and privacy are further provided by exterior cedar blinds.

Building Type: Residential
Construction Type: New Construction and Renovation
Size: 8,500 sf (790 sm)

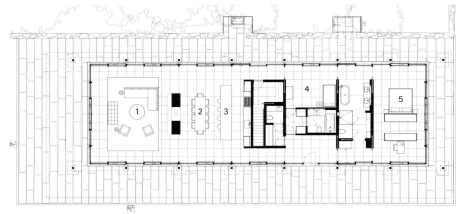

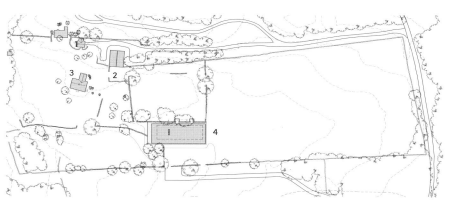

0 4' 8'   16'

Main-Level Plan

1 Living Room
2 Dining Room
3 Kitchen
4 Bedroom
5 Master Bedroom

0 10' 25'   50'

Site Plan

1 Existing Cabin
2 Reconstructed Barn
3 Restored Cottage
4 New House

Martha's Vineyard Residence

Museum of Contemporary Art San Diego

The Museum of Contemporary Art San Diego (MCASD) in La Jolla traces its origins to philanthropist Ellen Browning Scripps. Her final home, a modern oceanfront dwelling completed in 1916 by Irving Gill, served as the museum's first location. Since opening in 1941, the museum has undergone three architecturally distinct expansions. Selldorf Architects was tasked with creating new architecture that would significantly increase gallery space and provide a more welcoming and clear entry while giving greater coherence to the site and enhancing the museum's connection to its spectacular coastal setting.

In order to balance the scale with the massing of the existing structure, the new addition comprises a series of smaller volumes. The design's solidity and materials, including cast-in-place concrete, travertine panels, and aluminum brise-soleils, create a harmonious contrast with the existing stucco building. An existing auditorium will receive a skylight and will be repurposed as a gallery with 20-foot (6-meter) ceilings. New galleries on two levels form a fluid sequence with terrazzo floors, a material that establishes continuity with the existing building. The hexagonal lattice roof structure incorporates skylights, providing diffused lighting, while the eastern-facing galleries are fenestrated to bring the site's distinct natural light and coastal views into the museum.

Building Type: Cultural
Construction Type: New Construction and Renovation
Size: 30,000 sf (2,787 sm)

Museum of Contemporary Art San Diego

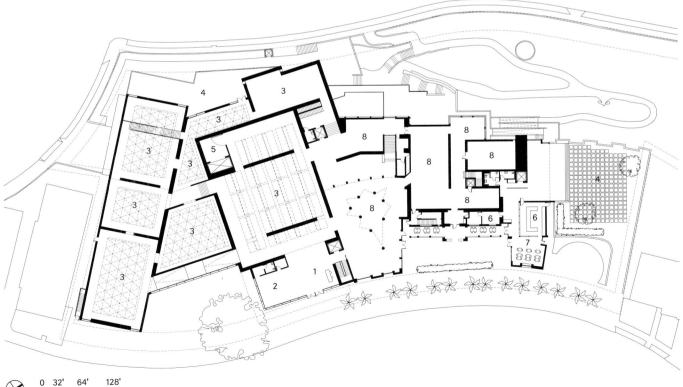

⊕ 0 32' 64' 128'

Main-Level Plan   4 Terrace
                       5 Loading Vestibule
1 Lobby   6 Kitchen
2 Bookstore   7 Café
3 New Gallery   8 Existing Gallery

Afterword

Annabelle Selldorf

This book chronicles projects we have worked on over the last fifteen years. Looking at them, I tried to formulate a thesis of what our architecture is about.

It is easy enough to enumerate themes: clarity of purpose, integrity of structure, proportion to volume, supremacy of light, restraint over gesture, longevity, and substance.

It is easy enough to speak of analytical process, of finding resolution that is rooted in a fundamental belief in the rational, the logical, and the explicable, and in humanist values and intelligence.

Apollo is the god of the rational.

It is harder to speak about the path of inspiration, the mind's eye—that which I believe is necessary to ultimately make architecture that matters. Surely it must be all of the above and in good measure: enough but not too much. But more than anything, it is the desire for all of it to come together to offer a moment of transcendence.

The search continues—ambiguity is a welcome tool; doubt is essential.

None of it would have any chance of realization if it were not for my wonderful partners, friends, and colleagues Sara Lopergolo, Lisa Green, Julie Hausch-Fen, Bill Bigelow, Eva Lemmer, and Barbara Lyle. We have worked together for many years, and I want to thank them for their talent, insight, creativity, thoughtfulness, and sense of humor.

My deep thanks go to a great and talented team of devoted architects and designers in the office. The ideas, the energy, and the spirit they bring to the work are immense.

I am extremely appreciative of our loyal and supportive clients, whose aspirations and ideas are paramount to the work.

Last and not least, I want to thank Todd Eberle, Ian Volner, Tom Eccles, and Wilvan Van Campen; Emilia Terragni and the entire Phaidon team; and Michael Bierut and Jessica Svendsen of Pentagram for the wonderful collaboration on this fine book.

Selldorf
Architects
Staff
1988–2015

Brian Aamoth
Leonie Adenauer
Victor Agran
Canan Akyuz
Jesse Algranti
Ross Amato
Eric Ansel
Joseph Arndt
Penelope August
Christaopher Baker
Gretchen Bank
Anna Barretto
Erin Bartling
Michael Baskett
Chaztity Beharry
David Bench
Safae Bendaoud
Lauren Benech
Aaron Bentley
Francine Besselaar
Alexandra Bethge
Beth Bevan
Cosimo Bicocchi
Bill Bigelow
Carlos Bisbal
Yaiza Blank
Anna Blume
Sandra Bohary
Celeste Booth-Clibborn
Laura Bown
Lisa Brandi
Mark Breeze
Christine Brennan
Ger Brennan
Zachary Brennan
Kirk Brown
Jill Brunstad
Anne Marie Burke
Kevin Cannon
Don Cantillo
Lilia Carrier
Lauren Caughley
Francesca Chang
Sarah Chatham
Jonathan Chesley
John Chow
Joy Christodoulides
Adrienne Colenburg
Angela Colley
Matthew Conrad
Dionisio Cortes Ortega
Estelle Courand
Brandon Crain
Zachary Crocker
Alison Cuthbert

J. Yolande Daniels
Darko de Franceschi
Julie de la Commune
Shyam Dharia
Jannis Dickel
Natalie Dowle
Nawal Elkhassasi
Rachael Elliott
Francine Elmquist
Raymond Eng
Lennie Ericksen
Dana Evan
Jeanie Fan
Diana Feigeles
Sondra Fein
Ryan FitzGerald
Paola Flores
Kerry Franses
Evelyn Freimann
Tobias Friedrich
Andreas Fuchs
Bernardo Garcia
Monica Gaura
Carrie Gibbs
Zachary Goldstein
Shirley Gouw
Randall Goya
Paul Granger
Leander Grayson Krueger
Catherine Green
Lisa Green
Matthew Green
Jennie Gruss
Julie Hanselmann Davies
Isabel Hanstein
Meredith Harris
Jasmin Hassan
Julie Hausch-Fen
Jack Hazan
Johannes Henkel
Paul Henkel
Jason Hernandez
Nigel Hetherington
Mary Hohlt
Lucas Hoffmann
Rachel Hoffman
Kate Houston
Katharine Huber
Pier Hughes
Chelsea Hyduk
Deidre Infante
Pranati Jain
James Jarzyniecki
Lindsay Johnson
Susan Johnson

Timothy Jones
Nicole Kamemoto-Lyons
Matthew Kanewske
Min Kang
Oscar Kang
Ryoji Karube
Kevin Keating
Diana Kellogg
Anna Kim
Jason Kim
Jin Yong Kim
Henriette Kockum
Annette Kortenbach
Whitney Kraus
Amity Kurt
Christina Kwak
Luis Laplace
Jaehyun Lee
Mark Leech
Eva Lemmer
Shlomit Levav
Lara Lightbody
Oliver Link
Celia Liu
Sara Lopergolo
Julia Lu
Karen Lu
Xander Lu
Alexis Luhrs
Barbara Lyle
Mimi Madigan
Kristine Makwinski
Maggie Mailer
Anna Maloney
Valerie Maltz Green
Julia Marani
Marco Marcellini
Andrea Martin
Sara Martin
Alexandra Martinec
Kevin McAlarnen
Stacy McAteer
Emma McGovern
Petra McKenzie
Elizabeth McNamara
Myriel Mechling
Oliver Menzi
Michele Messina
Noah Miller
Jessica Misuri
Friedrich Moeller
Philipp Mohr
Mariam Mojdehi
Filippo Mondadori
Marita Montes

David Moore
Granger Moorhead
Ivan Morales
Len Morgan
Nadja Müller
Sulekha Naidu
Michael Ness
Jean-Gabriel Neukonn
Anne Nixon
Rebecca Nordmann
Giulia Notaro
Thomas Offord
Chandler Oldham
Ian Ollivier
Jeanette Orlić
Brian O'Sullivan
Joshua Padgett
Crysta Pamphille
Susan Parapetti
Mary Patera
Chris Payne
Betty Perkin
Marc Pittsley
Jonathan Pohl
José Politi
Kathrin Presser-Velder
Julia Rafflenbeul
Richard Rapoport
Aaron Raymond
Laura Reid
Sarah Reilly
Stephan Repges
Andrew Reyniak
Parisa Rezaei-Abyaneh
Michelle Riboldi
Jeffrey Richards
Mary Richardson
Florian Rickenbacher
Melissa Rivers
Rachel Robinson
José Rodriguez
Elizabeth Rogoff
Danielle Romano
Cristina Rosa Cervello
Angelica Rosado
André Rösch
Elizabeth Rosenberg
Richard Round-Turner
Kathryn Rouse
Zachary Rousou
Amie Sachs
Yasser Salomon
Laura Samul
Lauren Sanford
Dylan Sauer

Katie Scallon
Heidi Schäfer
Bryan Scheib
Anniken Schmidt
Bernhard Schneider
Matthew Schnepf
Gerald Schriebl
Scott Schwarzwalder
Rebecca Seamans
Jacob Segal
Annabelle Selldorf
Cillian Sheehan
Vanessa Signer
Karishma Singapuri
Francesca Singer
Joe Smith
Wei Song
John Spencer
Christian Stanke
Stefan Steil
Jonathan Stitelman
Gretchen Stoecker
Jessica Strangward
Eleanor Strutt
James Stull
Jason Sudik
Wayne Switzer
Cassandra Tai-Marcellini
Cory Taylor
Warren Techentin
Danh Thai
Roshani Thakore
Ashley Theobalds
Nancy Thiel
Marc Thomas
Dominique Trotter
Jeanette Trudeau
Edward Tuck
Christine Van Deusen
Caroline Van Horn
Marina van Santen
Pargev Vardanian
Phil Veall
Nicholas Venezia
David Villar
Tanja Villbrandt
Jelene Vojvodič
Christian Volkmann
Franziska von Elverfeldt
Sylke Vonk
Alice von Stauffenberg
Byram Wadia
Yichen Wang
Lauren Wegel
Molly White

Elizabeth Wieber
Ewen Will
Christopher Williams
Wanda Willmore
Jessica Wilsey
Cynthia Wilson
Karl Wimmer
Susan Wines
Lennart Wolff
Marley Wright
Jiali Xuan
Bryan Yang
Susan Yun
Andrea Zaff
Besa Zajmi
Dawn Zingali
Monica Zwirner

Great appreciation and admiration
is due to all of the talented and
dedicated individuals who have
worked at Selldorf Architects.

Staff

Index

Image
Credits

Every reasonable attempt has been made to identify owners of copyright. Errors and omissions notified to the Publisher will be corrected in subsequent editions.

Portfolio

Todd Eberle: 19, 20, 21, 22–23, 24, 25, 26–27, 28, 29, 30, 31, 32, 33, 34–35, 37, 38, 40–41, 42–43, 44, 45, 46, 47, 48–49, 52, 53, 54, 55, 56–57, 58–59, 60, 61, 62, 64–65, 67, 68, 69, 70, 71, 73, 74–75, 76–77, 79, 80–81, 82, 83, 84–85, 86, 86, 90, 94, 95, 96, 97, 98, 100, 101, 102–103, 104–105, 106–107, 108, 109, 110, 111, 113, 114–115, 116–117, 118; Todd Eberle, Martin Creed, Work No. 1461, 2013, 2-inch wide adhesive tapes, Overall dimensions variable, © Martin Creed, Courtesy the artist and Hauser & Wirth: 39; Todd Eberle © Richard Serra / Artists Rights Society (ARS), New York, Courtesy David Zwirner New York London: 50–51, 91; Mark Bradford, Untitled, 2012, Etching, photogravure and chine-collé, Suite of 14 prints, 50.8 x 40.6 cm / 20 x 16 inches each, © Mark Bradford, Courtesy the artist and Hauser & Wirth, Photo: Todd Eberle: 63; Todd Eberle, Installation view, Mark Bradford: Be Strong Boquan, Hauser & Wirth New York, 18th Street, 2015, © Mark Bradford, Courtesy the artist and Hauser & Wirth: 88–89; Todd Eberle, Courtesy Neue Galerie New York: Museum for German and Austrian Art, Austrian permanent collection, installation by John Vinci, Gustav Klimt, The Dancer, c. 1916–18: 92–93; Todd Eberle © 2105 De Wain Valentine / Artists Rights Society (ARS), New York, Courtesy David Zwirner New York London: 99.

Projects

Mike Agee: 215 (t); Marino Auriti, Encyclopedic Palace of the World, ca. 1950s, 55th International Art Exhibition, The Encyclopedic Palace, The Venice Biennale, Photo by

Francesco Galli, Courtesy La Biennale di Venezia: 191 (t); Ettore Bellini: 168, 169, 170 (bl, br), 171; Roberto Cuoghi, Belinda, 2013, 55th International Art Exhibition, The Encyclopedic Palace, The Venice Biennale, Photo by Francesco Galli, Courtesy La Biennale di Venezia: 191 (b); Alex Delfanne, © 2015 Fred Sandback Archive, Courtesy David Zwirner, New York / London: 172 (t), 173 (tl); © The Easton Foundation, Licensed by VAGA, Courtesy Hauser & Wirth, Photo by Peter Mallet: 156 (c, b), 157; Todd Eberle: 146, 147 (br), 148, 149 (tl), 150, 151, 152, 162, 163, 174, 175 (tl, tc, b), 200, 201, 208 (br); 210 (b); 228, 229, 230, 231 (tl, tr), 232, 233, 235 (tl, tr); Todd Eberle, Courtesy Neue Galerie New York: Museum for German and Austrian Art, Bauhaus Permanent Collection, Installation by John Vinci: 129 (c,b), 133 (t); Todd Eberle, Courtesy Neue Galerie New York: Museum for German and Austrian Art: 131 (tl); Todd Eberle, Courtesy Neue Galerie New York: Museum for German and Austrian Art, Austrian Permanent Collection, Installation by John Vinci, Gustav Klimt, The Dancer, c. 1916–18: 131 (b); Todd Eberle, Courtesy Neue Galerie New York: Museum for German and Austrian Art, Egon Schiele, Portrait of the Painter Karl Zakovsek, 1910, Adolf Loos, Knieschwimmer Club Chair, c. 1930: 131 (tr); Todd Eberle Artwork © Estate of John McCracken: 138 (t); Todd Eberle, Zwirner & Wirth, 69th Street, New York, NY, 2001, Foreground: Bruce Nauman, 'Large Butt to Butt,' 1989, Background: Bruce Nauman, 'Four Pairs of Heads,' 1991 © 2015 Bruce Nauman / Artists Rights Society (ARS), New York: 147 (t); Adam Friedberg, Courtesy Neue Galerie New York: Museum for German and Austrian Art: 130 (tl, tr, br); Adam Friedberg © Matthew Day Jackson 178 (b); Adam Friedberg © Dieter Roth Estate 179 (t); Courtesy of Gagosian Gallery, Photography by Prudence Cuming Associates Ltd., © 2015 Estate of Pablo Picasso / Artists Right Society (ARS), New York: 154,

155 (t); © Jeff Goldberg/Esto: 212, 213, 214, 215 (b), 216 (t); Uli Grohs: 140, 141, 142, 143 (tl, tr); Courtesy of Hauser & Wirth, Photo by Alex Delfanne: 156 (t); Courtesy Hauser & Wirth, Genevieve Hanson: 176 (c); Ken Hayden: 164, 165, 166, 167 (t); Hervé Hôte: 222 (c, b), 224 (br); Hypertecture Studio, Inc.: 216 (b); Warren Jagger: 204, 205, 206, 207 (t); Hans Josephsohn, Untitled, particolare dell'Installazione, Arsenale, 55th International Art Exhibition, The Encyclopedic Palace, The Venice Biennale, Photo by Francesco Galli, Courtesy of La Biennale di Venezia: 190 (b); Hulya Kolabas: 129 (tc), 130 (bl); Nikolas Koenig: 136 (t, c), 138 (t), 144 (t), 147 (bl), 181 (cl), 192 (t), 193, 194 (b), 195 (b), 196, 208 (t), 209, 210 (tl, tr); Nikolas Koenig © 2015 Anish Kapoor/ Artists Rights Society (ARS), New York, 145 (t, br); Nikolas Koenig © the artists: 136 (bl, br), 138 (b), 139; Marc Lins: 192 (c), 195 (t), 297; Thomas Loof / Trunk Archive: 162 (bl, br); John Majoris: 194 (t); © Paul McCarthy, Courtesy the artist and Hauser & Wirth, Genevieve Hanson: 176 (b); John Outterbridge, Déjà-Vu-Do, 1970–92, 55th International Art Exhibition, The Encyclopedic Palace, The Venice Biennale, Photo by Francesco Galli, Courtesy of La Biennale di Venezia: 190 (t); David Regen, © 2015 Anish Kapoor/Artists Rights Society (ARS), New York: 145 (bl); © Dieter Roth Estate, Courtesy Hauser & Wirth, Bjarni Grímsson: 178 (t); Shinichi Sawada, Untitled, 2006–7, 55th International Art Exhibition, The Encyclopedic Palace, The Venice Biennale, Photo by Francesco Galli, Courtesy of La Biennale di Venezia: 190 (c); Jason Schmidt: 182 (t), 183 (t), 184 (tl, tr, cr), 187 (t); Jason Schmidt, © 2015 John Chamberlain / Artists Rights Society (ARS), New York, NY: 182 (b); Jason Schmidt, © 2015 Stephen Flavin / Artists Rights Society (ARS), New York, NY: 185, 186; Jason Schmidt, © Judd Foundation. Licensed by VAGA, New York, NY: 182 (c), 184 (b); Jason Schmidt, © Judd Foundation. Licensed by VAGA,

New York, NY, © 2015 Richard Serra / Artists Rights Society (ARS), New York, NY, © 2015 Fred Sandback Archive: 187 (b); Courtesy of Selldorf Architects: 132, 133 (b), 134, 135, 137 (b), 143 (b), 144 (bl, br), 149 (tr, bl, bc, br), 153, 155 (b), 167 (b), 170 (tr), 172 (b), 175 (tr), 176 (t), 177, 179 (b), 180, 181 (tl, tr, cr, b), 183 (b), 188, 189, 192 (b), 198, 199, 202, 203, 207 (b), 208 (bl), 211, 217, 218, 219, 220, 221, 222 (t), 223, 224 (t, bl), 225, 226, 227, 231 (b), 235 (b), 239 (b), 240, 241, 242, 243, 244, 245, 246, 247; © David Sundberg | Esto: 158, 159, 160, 161 (t); VUW Studio: 234, 236, 237, 238, 239 (t); Stephen White: 173 (tr); Stephen White, Courtesy David Zwirner, New York / London and Zeno X Gallery, Antwerp: 173 (c, b).

Phaidon Press Limited
Regent's Wharf
All Saints Street
London N1 9PA

Phaidon Press Inc.
65 Bleecker Street
New York, NY 10012

phaidon.com

First published 2016
© 2016 Phaidon Press Limited

ISBN 978 0 7148 7117 2

A CIP catalogue record for
this book is available from
the British Library and the
Library of Congress.

Selldorf Architects
Editorial Team:
Lisa J. Green, Lilia Carrier,
Sara Martin

Commissioning Editor:
Emilia Terragni

Project Editor:
Laura Loesch-Quintin

Production Controllers:
Nerissa Vales, Sue Medlicott

Design: Pentagram

Printed in China